• A REGAL BIBLE COMMENTARY FOR LAYMEN •

STUART BRISCOE

Purifying the Church

What God Expects of You and Your Church

A Topical Commentary on Titus

Regal Books

A Division of GL Publications
Ventura, California, U.S.A.

Published by Regal Books
A Division of GL Publications
Ventura, California 93006
Printed in U.S.A.

1 2 3 4 5 6 7 8 9 10 / 91 90 89 88 87

Library of Congress Cataloging-in-Publication Data

Briscoe, D. Stuart.
    Purifying the church: a topical commentary on Titus / by D. Stuart Briscoe.
        p.   cm.
    ISBN 0-8307-1246-1 : $7.95
    1. Bible. N.T. Titus—Commentaries.   I. Title.
    BS2755.3.B75   1987   87-21002
    227'.8107 dc19   CIP

Rights for publishing this book in other languages are contracted by Gospel
Literature International (GLINT) foundation. GLINT also provides technical
help for the adaptation, translation, and publishing of Bible study resources
and books in scores of languages worldwide. For further information, contact
GLINT, Post Office Box 488, Rosemead, California, 91770, U.S.A., or the
publisher.

Contents

Introduction

The Epistle to Titus is one of the shortest books of the Bible and, accordingly, has been somewhat overlooked. This is unfortunate because despite its brevity, the depth and significance of its teaching cannot be overstated, and its special relevance for today's Church should not be underestimated.

Titus was one of the men into whom Paul had poured his life and with whom he had shared his ministry. This in itself serves to give us a necessary model for the sort of relationship that can and should develop between Christian leaders and the next generation who will assume their mantles.

All too often flourishing works of grace wither on the vine when those whom God used to initiate them leave the scene devoid of adequate leadership under which God will perpetuate the work. Sometimes this is due to the attitude of the leader, who for some reason is unable or unwilling to allow others into an intimacy of relationship that will serve to pass on the heartbeat and experience of the one to the other. Where this is true the Church of Jesus Christ is inevitably impoverished. Paul not only reminds us that

those of the next generation are one of our best invest-
ments, but he also shows practically how to do the invest-
ing.

Leadership is clearly one of the pressing concerns of
any church and not least in this generation. There is
always a price to pay by those who aspire under God to be
the leaders of His Church. This price has a higher tag than
many today are prepared to pay. So, for instance, it is not
uncommon to find people entering the ministry whose first
questions of prospective churches are related to time off,
salary, sabbatical and the number of hours expected of
them in any one workweek.

A careful reading of the Apostle's correspondence with
men such as Titus, who ministered in Crete, and Timothy,
who was engaged in similar ministry in Ephesus, should
set the record straight. But Paul's vision of leadership was
by no means confined to the somewhat narrow limits of
professionalism into which it has often been pressed in the
contemporary Church. The elders were a major concern
of Paul's, and the instructions given to Titus, as to the cali-
ber of people who were suitable candidates and the type of
ministry they would be embarking upon, serve as
extremely valuable resources in our efforts to develop
elders in the modern Church.

With the proliferation of means of communication,
there has come a proliferation of messages and a parallel
proliferation of confusion. It is not at all unusual for even
the most well-meaning believers to become bogged down
in all manner of confounding and controversial issues as
they tune in to one preacher after another through books,
tapes, radio and television. Considerable maturity is
required both in biblical knowledge and social skills if the
confusion is to be cleared up. Solid teaching, practical
application, personalized training are all required, and Paul

recognized this in his ministry and instructed Titus in the necessity to make it available to the people of the infant churches.

Then there is the major problem of motivating the church members. People in North America and other developed countries have a remarkable capacity for over-extending themselves. Sometimes this is because they have chosen a standard of living that has become a tyrannical master of their time, energy and devotion. Other times it is simply because having become free to try anything, they have assumed they must now become proficient at everything. The result is that motivating God's people to sacrificial, consistent and faithful service has become an art and a science for which many leaders are not particularly well-equipped. Here again, Paul is wonderfully helpful.

Nobody who is normal relishes the idea of having to confront people about their wrongdoing and institute appropriate action that will produce solutions acceptable to all concerned. Because it is particularly difficult to function in this manner in the Church, the work of Church discipline is often left undone. Titus was reminded of the seriousness of this omission and in a very straightforward manner was given directions he was expected to follow and which we would do well to heed.

In short, Titus was told how to work in a church so that it would function well and become recognizable in the local environment as the "people of God." While many pew packers have differing views of what the Church is and, accordingly, what it is supposed to be doing, there are still many influential people in the pulpits and the pews who recognize the unique and noble position the local church fills in the plan and economy of God. In addition, they are deeply committed to work hard to see that as much as it depends on them God might be free to work in, with and through them to the purifying of His people. This book was written by one who shares this concern.

Now a personal word. There came a time in the church in which my wife and I have been honored to serve for over 16 years when the structures of leadership were in danger of collapsing under their own weight. They were wonderfully adequate when the church was founded with a handful of people some 25 years earlier, but were woefully threadbare for a church with approximately 5,000 people in attendance. So something had to be done to institute change. I had been in the pastorate long enough to know that change is not popular because it is uncomfortable and threatening, and I also knew that unless there was a biblical base for the proposals, they would not even get to first base. So I decide to embark on a series of simple expositions of Paul's letter to Titus for a period of eight consecutive Sunday mornings.

It was encouraging to see how the congregation became increasingly involved in the teaching and progressively open to the application of the proposed changes in constitution and church leadership. This is not to suggest that all it took to effect radical change was a series of sermons! Far from it. It took hours of discussion and debate and many months of careful preparation before the changes were effected so well that to the best of my knowledge only one family departed the scene in protest. The sermons were extremely relevant to our situation and were, therefore, delivered with no small dose of passion and intensity.

Because this book has been prepared from transcribed versions of the spoken word and because we want to retain something of the fervor with which the messages were delivered, we have retained much of the rhetoric, the repetition, the outlines and other devices that are more appropriate to spoken than written communication. We trust, however, that this, rather than serving to distract, will serve only to help the reader catch the spirit of what was being said and realize that these are the words of a pastor talking to his beloved people, as together they work at what it means to be the people of God in "Old Milwaukee."

CHAPTER ONE

Identifying God's People

I. The calling of the people of God

A. God chose Israel as His people

1. To model community
2. To show His sovereignty
3. To exhibit His grace
4. To identify His solemnity

B. God chose Christ as His Stone

1. Cornerstone
2. Capstone
3. Stumbling stone

C. God chose us as His Church

1. That we may glorify Him
2. To do that which is good

II. The characteristics of the people of God

A. People of faith

1. Justified by faith
2. Live by faith

B. People of knowledge

1. Know the truth
2. Acknowledge the truth

C. People of hope

1. In a God who does not lie
2. In promises that never fail

Titus 1:1-4

Paul, a servant of God and an apostle of Jesus Christ for the faith of God's elect and the knowledge of the truth that leads to godliness—a faith and knowledge resting on the hope of eternal life, which God, who does not lie, promised before the beginning of time, and at his appointed season he brought his word to light through the preaching entrusted to me by the command of God our Savior, to Titus, my true son in our common faith: Grace and peace from God the Father and Christ Jesus our Savior.

At first sight these initial four verses of the apostle Paul's letter to Titus do not hold any great promise because they're simply a traditional formal opening to a letter. In the days in which Paul was writing, it was customary for the writer to introduce himself first and, second, to state the person to whom he was writing, and then, to give formal traditional greetings. So Paul's Epistle fits into the traditional formal pattern.

But there is a difference. Paul takes all this traditional formality and invests it with a specific significance. For instance, he doesn't just say "Paul." He says, "Paul, a servant of God and an apostle of Jesus Christ," and goes on for three verses. He doesn't just say "Titus," the person to whom he's writing. But in a beautiful succinct statement he calls him "my genuine child in the faith that we share together."

As far as the formal greetings are concerned, "grace and peace" were normal greetings; but you'll notice that Paul invests them with deep significance. For the grace and peace that he's talking about emanate "from God the Father and Christ Jesus our Savior."

So already we have the clue that this formal traditional greeting is something of deep importance.

Now, the purpose of the letter is not included in these four verses but in the fifth one. Paul and Titus have been on an evangelistic mission to Crete. Paul moved on and wrote to Titus explaining, "The reason I left you in Crete was that you might straighten out what was left unfinished and appoint elders in every town, as I directed you."

The apostle Paul was not just interested in evangelizing so that individuals could come to personal relationship with Christ. That, of course, was the start. But then he was interested in taking these new converts and forming fellowships, churches, "in every town" in Crete.

Paul told Titus to "straighten out what was left unfinished," specifically to develop the structure of the church. To do this, Titus is given the responsibility to personally appoint elders in every town. So, Titus's particular ministry is to pick up the fruits of evangelism, form them into bodies of believers in all the different towns all over Crete and establish churches. It's what we call, in contemporary jargon, a church-planting ministry. It is, of course, a very important aspect of all ministry.

However, while the idea of straightening out what was left unfinished in appointing elders in every church is the human side of what was being done, Paul points out the divine aspect of what is going on. In Titus 2:14 he says, speaking of our Lord Jesus, that he "Gave himself for us to redeem us from all wickedness and to purify for himself a people that are his very own, eager to do what is good."

When Titus goes to the different towns around Crete and establishes churches, that's the human side of it, the practical side. But the divine and spiritual side of it is that God is purifying a people that are His very own. Put those two things together and you'll discover something very important: The ministry of the gospel requires that when we bring people to Christ, we introduce them to a fellowship of believers that takes seriously the fact that they are to be God's very own people in their geographic locations.

We're going to examine this Epistle to find out what it really means to be not only related to Christ, but in that relationship to be related to those who are Christ's and to be a member of God's very own people in a specific geographic location. God's very own people then is the theme of this book based on Paul's letter to Titus.

The Calling of the People of God

In the introduction Paul says he is "A servant of God and an apostle of Jesus Christ for the faith of God's elect." Notice that little expression "God's elect." The word *elect* means "to choose," and Scripture shows quite clearly that God is in the habit of electing, or choosing. Now, whenever we think in terms of God's elect, we think in terms of a people that God has called, a people He has chosen for Himself. The basis of this, of course, is found in the Old Testament, where on numerous occasions we read of God choosing a people for Himself (see Exod. 19:5; Deut. 7:6; 14:2).

God Chose Israel as His People

The Israelites were not chosen to be God's people because they were special; they were not chosen because they were perfect; they were not chosen because they were strong. They were chosen because they were chosen. In other words, the choice rests with God Himself.

But behind the choice of Israel as a people is another choice: God's choice to have a people at all. Why does He want a people in the first place? We might well ask that question when we remember the hassles God had with His people, Israel. But I think the answer is very important.

God is anxious to produce communities of people who are readily identifiable, in a special sense, as His people. Why? We need to remember that in the beginning God created man. After He created man He left him for a little while, and then decided man couldn't make it on his own. So God had a wonderful idea: He created woman.

When God created man He created an individual. As soon as God created woman, He created community, or society. Then disaster fell. Man fell, and community also began to fall apart. Man and woman had a beautiful relationship that promptly deteriorated. Not only that, they produced children, and the first one they produced was a murderer and the second was the brother he murdered. In other words, community—society—promptly began to disintegrate.

Now, God had created man who fell, and God had created society that fragmented. The questions we need to ask ourselves are: So what? Does God care? Yes, we know that God certainly cares about fallen man. How much does He care? He cared enough to send Christ to be the Savior of fallen mankind.

But, does God care about fragmented society? Yes, He

does. He has ordained that those fallen men who are redeemed by Christ should be part of an alternate society, a new, readily identifiable community. And that community, that alternate society, is called *the church,* the people of God, God's elect, those who are particularly His.

The first reason God chose a people was so that they might live as a *model community* in the midst of fragmentation to show what community is all about. He called Israel and made them a nation. Then He placed them as a nation and a people in the midst of other nations and said to them, "Okay, now show the nations how nations behave when God is the Lord."

The second reason God chose a people for Himself, of course, was that He wanted to make it very clear that He was *the sovereign Lord,* that He would act as He chose. And He demonstrated this on numerous occasions with His people. Their history is one long story of God's sovereign intervention in their affairs. Perhaps the best-known illustration is when they were brought out of Egypt in that massive Exodus; when, in a remarkable way, God stretched forth His mighty arm and delivered them out of the hands of the Egyptians. Whenever you read about Israel's history, you will find that God's chosen people constantly refer to the Exodus as a sovereign act of God. It is a basic plank of their history, something that is deeply important to them.

God, then, calls the people to Himself, first, in order that they might be a model of community and, second, that they might be the means of showing His sovereignty.

Third, *God's people are also to be the means of demonstrating His grace.* Over and over again God dealt with His own in a way they didn't deserve. He showered His blessings upon them even when they were ungrateful, even when they were rebellious to Him. For instance, in the

God chose a people . . .
so that they might live as a
model community in the
midst of fragmentation."

wilderness He showers manna, bread from heaven, upon them on a daily basis. But they are a grumbling people; they are disgruntled; they are wishing they were back in Egypt; they are doubting their leadership; they are schismatic; they are just a nasty bunch of people, yet God says, "I won't give you what you deserve; I'll give you the manna you don't deserve."

Fourth, God chose a people in order that He might clearly identify *the solemnity* of being related to Him.

Even though these people were His elect, even though He had chosen them to be His people, that didn't mean it all came about automatically. His people had all kinds of responsibilities, and He told them, "Either you do it my way, or you're in trouble." They didn't do it His way; they finished up in trouble. He warned them repeatedly through the prophets of the possibility of exile; they didn't heed His warning. And the elect people, the chosen people, demonstrated categorically that you don't mess around with God. Because they did not do it God's way, but followed their own paths, the chosen people did go into terrible exile. They were dispersed around the world, as a consequence of their own sin and their own disobedience.

So God had His elect people. He chose them so that, in His dealings with them, they might learn and teach other nations some things about God.

God Chose Christ as His Stone

Today, God's elect people are the Church. We are the chosen of God by virtue of our relationship with His Son, Jesus Christ. In 1 Peter 2:4 we read: "As you come to him [the Lord Jesus], the living Stone—rejected by men but chosen [here's the word elect again—chosen or elect] by God and precious to him—you also, like living stones, are being built into a spiritual house to be a holy priesthood."

Using the picture of Christ as the stone, the chosen one of God, Peter then shows in verse 6 how He is the cornerstone, the capstone in verse 7, the stumbling stone in verse 8. Jesus was chosen by God to function in this capacity.

The *cornerstone* is the base upon which everything is built; the foundation. The *capstone* is the locking stone that makes everything hold together. The *stumbling stone* is that over which people trip if they don't treat it properly. This is what Christ was chosen to be. He was chosen to be the foundation of everything that God is doing for man. He was chosen to be the capstone who makes everything in God's dealings with man make sense and hold together. He is the foundation and the basis of everything God wants to do, if men will respond. But if they won't respond, they will find that He will be the one against whom they will bark their shins and skin their knees and bang their noses; they will stumble over Him and find Him an offense.

God Chose Us as His Church

In Ephesians 1:4 Paul talks about the Church, the people of God. He talks about those who are in Christ: "For he [God] chose us in him before the creation of the world to be holy and blameless in his sight." These people who are the Church, who are in Christ, who are the Body of Christ, God also calls "the elect," the special people of God. God has chosen that the Church in today's world should be His people, His very own people. It is terribly important that believers understand the significance of the Body of Christ and what it means to be in Christ.

Our problem is that we are very individualized in our

lives and in our thinking. This flows over into our spiritual experience, which often is on a very limited, individualized basis. But that doesn't go far enough. We are to understand ourselves to be not only individuals related to Christ, but individuals related to those related to Christ. Those in a visible, tangible body known specifically as the people of God, God's elect people in that particular place, the church.

One of the problems many of us have is that we say what I used to say in my late teens and early 20s: "I'm all in favor of Jesus Christ, but as far as His Church is concerned, forget it." I remember applauding with great enthusiasm when I saw a movie in which the young Cliff Richards was talking to the vicar of a church. This young kid said to the stereotypical English Anglican vicar: "If I was Jesus Christ and came back to earth and saw what you'd done to my church, I'd sue you." And I clapped with everybody else. We thought that was absolutely great, because the easiest thing in the world to do is to knock the Church. Anybody who can't knock the Church has simply chloroformed his critical capabilities. All you have to remember is that the Church is made up exclusively of sinners, so anybody who can't find fault with it just isn't trying.

But, we don't have the freedom to casually criticize the Church, and I'll tell you why. Because the Church of Jesus Christ is a community of people in Christ, the Body of Christ, the chosen of God, the people of God, God's very own people, placed in geographic locations to *be* something and to *do* something. This is our calling. It's a noble calling; it's a frightening calling; but it's our calling, nevertheless.

The apostle Paul says that those of us who are chosen in Christ, and are the Body of Christ, are called "To the praise of his glorious grace" (Eph. 1:6). Now, that doesn't mean that we as individuals—what we are—glorifies Him. It means that what we are as a community *glorifies Him.* That's why, you see, it's such a hassle being part of the Church of Jesus Christ. It is a tremendously demanding calling—not just individually to be to His glory, but collectively, to behave ourselves as a community, as a fellowship, in a way that glorifies Him.

It isn't just what we are, it's also what we do. As we have already pointed out, Titus 2:14 says that the people who are His very own are eager to do what is good. We are a people characterized by what we are, which is to the praise of His glory, and what we do, *that which is good* by His standards of goodness.

So the apostle Paul sends Titus on a very simple mission. He says, "All right. Go into every town in Crete and establish churches there from the products of our evangelism. Ordain elders in every place and straighten out what needs to be straightened out. And always remember, Titus, as you are straightening out the practical details of these churches, you are actually making it possible for Christ to purify for Himself His very own people in those towns."

What an exciting concept that, in every town in Crete, it will be possible to identify God's very own people. What an exciting thought to think that in your city or town today you can identify God's very own people. Wherever we go around the world we can identify God's very own people. That is what we are called to. It is not just a lot of individuals; it is a community of people knit together as the Body of Christ, God's called people, His very own.

I want to pause here and ask some questions. Do you understand the significance of what it means to be identified with Christ and then to identify with a church? If you understand the significance of what it means to be identified with the Lord Jesus, then are you openly willing to commit yourself to His people? That is, to throw your weight with that people so you can be to His glory and do what is good and be clearly identifiable in your geographic location as a member of God's very own people. Have you done that? Or are you keeping your spiritual experience personal? Are you keeping yourself peripheral? Have you determined that as little involvement as possible is the way to go?

I remember somebody once telling me, when I said something about the church, "Well, you've got to understand, Stuart, we aren't joiners; we never join anything." But, fortunately, they began to listen to Scripture and discovered that if you identify with Christ, you are called to identify with God's very own people.

The Characteristics of the People of God

Now, if this very own people are to be readily identifiable as such in a specific geographic location, it seems reasonable to ask, What are the characteristics of these people? What is it that helps identify them? Paul tells us in his formal, traditional, but expanded greeting. He says that he is "A servant of God and an apostle of Jesus Christ" for three reasons: First, "for the faith of God's elect"; second, for "the knowledge of the truth that leads to godliness"; and third, for "the hope of eternal life, which God, who does not lie, promised before the beginning of time."

How do we identify the people of God? First, they're people of faith; second, they're people of knowledge; third, they are people of hope—and all these not just as individuals, but as a community.

People of Faith

God's very own people are people of faith in the sense that they know what it is to be justified by faith. Everybody who believes in God would like to be right with God eventually. A lot of people who believe in God want to delay it until as late as possible. They want to do their own thing and then get right with God at the last possible minute. But that simply shows how little they understand God.

People who are serious about God want to be right with God, and there are two basic ways they think they can do it. One is to "do your best and hope for the best." The problem with this concept is that everyone disagrees with what is best. There is a problem with the definition. If these people say you get right with God by doing your best, and you try to nail them down a bit, they'll say that keeping the Ten Commandments, living by the Sermon on the Mount and following the Golden Rule are examples of "doing your best."

I have spent time talking with people who advocate these approaches and I've noticed that none of them have ever been able to show me where in the Bible the Ten Commandments are; none of them could tell me which Gospel the Sermon on the Mount is in; and none of them could quote the Golden Rule. In other words, a lot of people who say the way you get right with God is by doing your best aren't really taking it seriously. If you try to do your best, hoping that it will make you right with God, number one, you won't do it, and number two, even if you did, it wouldn't be good enough.

The second way people think they can get right with God is not on the basis of doing their best and earning it, but in admitting that their best isn't good enough. They admit openly to the Lord, "I am unhealthy, inadequate and a rebellious sinful person. I deserve only your righteous indignation, but I understand that you offer graciously what I don't deserve and I ask for this gracious provision and accept all you offer in grateful faith."

The people of faith are the people who don't talk a lot of nonsense about getting right with God by doing their best. The people of faith are those who say the only way you can get right with God is by asking Him graciously to give them what they don't deserve, for Christ's sake, and then by faith receive it. It's what the Bible calls "being justified by grace" (Titus 3:7) through faith. Now, the people of God, those who are God's very own people, know they have been *justified by faith*. That's why churches ask those who come to join if they can testify to the fact that they have been saved by grace through faith. If they can't, they haven't even started to be people of faith.

Remember, that you start as a person of faith by being justified by faith, but then you go on from there. You *live by faith*. Dr. Carl Henry made a powerful statement: "A disconcertingly wide segment of American society succumbs to the premise that life has not come from God, does not move towards God, and cannot be enriched by God."[1] That's basically the philosophy of our society.

We call ourselves a Christian nation; we talk about the founding fathers until we go blue in the face; we come up with all kinds of highfalutin and high-sounding statements about getting prayer back in the schools and whatnot. But what we're really confronting in this society is a wide segment of people who frankly don't believe that life came from God or is moving toward God or can be enriched by God; in other words, God is utterly irrelevant.

Now then, if that's the society as a whole, do you see how easy it is to be a person of faith and to stand out among them? Because you see, if you believe by faith that

God's very own people know they have been justified by faith."

you came from God and that you're going to God and are answerable to Him, and you believe by faith that every single day God can intervene in your affairs by His Spirit, through His Word and in the fellowship of believers that enriches your life, you will stick out like a sore thumb in this faithless generation.

Now, what is a community of believers? A community of believers is a visible, tangible body of believers in a specific situation, comprised of people of faith. Are you a person of faith? Have you been justified by faith? Do you get up in the morning and thank God that you've come from Him and you're going to Him and you're living unto Him? Do you simply open up your life to His intervention, reckon with His grace and count on His presence, and live in the life and the glory of His being? That's faith. Let's face it, God's very own people are people of faith.

People of Knowledge

Second, God's very own people are people of knowledge. He says that they are the people who have *knowledge of the truth* that leads to godliness. Now knowledge of the truth means, first of all, that they have accumulated data. They have their facts right about the truth of God, or, to put it another way, they have taken time out to learn their theology.

One of the things that concerns me about the contemporary Church in North America is that we are more experience-oriented than theology-oriented. For instance, if you look at the books people buy, you will find that a high percentage are experience-oriented books: How can I feel better? How can I look better? How can I sort my marriage out? How can I sort my kids out? How am I going to be or feel or look or do better?

Then look at how many people buy books of theology—on the person of God, the person of Christ, the person of the Holy Spirit, the theology of man, the theology of the last times, the theology of the Church. You will discover that the wide majority of people in the Christian community don't study at all, and a wide selection of those who do study are committed exclusively to experience-oriented study. People who really take time to get a knowledge of the truth are a small minority. Now, this is a concern. When the apostle Paul says that the people of God are people of knowledge, however, he is not just talking about people who know truth. He is talking about people who know truth to the point of acknowledging the truth. The Greek word he uses is *epignōsis*, which means "to know thoroughly and to acknowledge what you know."

I know that Elizabeth is the Queen of the United Kingdom. But if she were to walk into the room, the fact that I know her would not necessarily mean that I would behave properly towards her. I might just sit down, stick my hands in my pockets, chew my gum and ignore her. I would know who she is, but I might not acknowledge who she is. If I were to acknowledge what I know, it would mean that I would stand up and quietly give attention to her, and treat her with respect. It doesn't mean I have to agree with her policies; it doesn't mean I have to like her as a person; what it means is that she is the Queen and I acknowledge her as such. It's one thing to know. It's another thing to acknowledge. *Epignōsis*, the knowledge of which Paul speaks, is *acknowledging the truth* that we know. And the people of God are people of knowledge—they know the truth and they are prepared to acknowledge in their lives the truth. These are the people of God, God's very own people.

But notice that Paul goes on to say that this knowledge of truth *leads to godliness.* The Greek word for "godliness" is *eusebeia,* which means literally "to tremble before God," or to treat Him with deep respect and utter reverence, or, to use the old-term expression that was discarded long ago, to have a great fear of God. That's what godliness really means. Now, part of our problem is that we have become on such intimate, friendly terms with God that He's a bit of a buddy. It's rather nice to have that intimate relationship with God and it's all very valid indeed, unless it brings us to the point of overlooking the fact that He is awesome.

A godly person is one who always has a sense of awe when he understands the majesty of God. A godly person comes always with a sense of trembling, because he knows that before the holiness of God man is utterly sinful himself. A person who is godly looks at the power of God and is overwhelmed by a sense of his own inadequacy. So, with a sense of awe, a sense of shame, and a sense of inadequacy, he comes humbly before his God with reverence and holy fear. That's what happens when you know and acknowledge the truth. It produces godliness.

God's very own people are people of faith. God's very own people are people of knowledge. Isaiah 66:2 sums this up magnificently. This is what the Lord declares: "This is the one I esteem: he who is humble and contrite in spirit, and trembles at my word." Who is the person that God esteems? "He who is humble and contrite in spirit, and trembles at my word." You members of the people of God are identified with a community of people that have a deep-down desire to be known in their towns as God's very own people. If this is so, what you are talking about is being a person of faith, a person of knowledge.

People of Hope

The apostle Paul goes on to say that he is a servant and an apostle for the "hope of eternal life, which God, who does not lie, promised before the beginning of time." He is saying, those who are identified with the living God are people who are characterized by hope. That hope is an overwhelming confidence, and it relates to eternal life. They believe that when the Scriptures say these things are written "That you may know that you have eternal life" (1 John 5:13), they are written to be believed.

I remember talking to somebody one day who said, "Do you think you have eternal life? Do you mean to stand there and tell me that you think you have eternal life?"

I said, "Yes, and I don't think it, I know it."

He said, "I think you're arrogant."

I said, "I can understand that."

He said, "Nobody, but nobody can know that they have eternal life."

So I said, "Now I think you're arrogant."

He said, "Why?"

I said, "Because you presume to know better than the Word of God. The Word of God says that these things are written that you may *know* that you *have* eternal life. And you know better. Who's arrogant? Somebody who believes the Word of God or somebody who knows better than the Word does?"

It is not arrogance to put your trust in Christ. It is not arrogance to come humbly and contritely before God and tremble at His Word. It is not arrogance to admit that you can't save yourself. It is not arrogance to come open-handed and empty-handed and brokenhearted before God and say, "Oh God, for Christ's sake, forgive me and give me what I don't deserve." That's not arrogance. That's common sense. And there are people who have come before the Lord and know that they have eternal life, and this has become their hope. This has become their confidence. Why? Because this eternal life was promised to them by a God who cannot and who does not lie. Norman J. Clayton entitled one of his great hymns, "My Hope Is in the Lord," the chorus of which emphasizes the theme that for me He died, for me He lives, and He freely gives everlasting life and light.[2] And what does that mean for all God's people? It means that life down here is tinted with the glow of life up there. It means that eternity invests itself into all our experiences of time. It means that the most mundane things of earth are touched with the glory of heaven.

I'll tell you something very exciting. There are people who are full of hope and people who are full of knowledge. There are also people who are full of faith. And they get together and become a church; they become an assembly; they become a visible, vital, viable entity in society—God's very own people.

I encourage you to be part of all this. One of the most crucial things that ever happened to me was when a very good friend of mine, a very well-known preacher, said to me after hearing me preach one time, "Stuart, the problem with your theology is it incorporates no ecclesiology." In other words, he was telling me everything I had to say was related to an individual's relationship with God. "But," he said, "there's a whole lot more to theology than that. What about the individual relationship to each other in the church, the community of believers?"

Ask yourself these questions. Do I take the Church of Jesus Christ seriously? Have I identified with the people of God? Can they count on me? Do they even know who I am? Do they know my faith? Do they know my knowledge? Do they know my hope? Does my faith, knowledge and hope engender faith, knowledge and hope in others? Does the faith, knowledge and hope of others encourage my faith, knowledge and hope? Am I part of those whom others know are God's very own people? Or am I just going it alone, making sure that I'm as uninvolved as possible in what it is God is committed to—the building of His Church.

Questions for further study _____

1. What was the apostle Paul's concern for leaving Titus in Crete following their evangelistic mission there? Can you see any reason for that same kind of concern today?
2. While Titus was at work on the human level "straightening out what was left unfinished," what was God in the process of doing? Can you see God at work today purifying His people?
3. List four reasons why God chose a people for His very own? How can you take each of these areas and relate what it means to you to be God's chosen. His elect?
4. What are the three characteristics that readily identify God's very own people in a specific geographic location? Do these characteristics readily identify you as one of God's very own in the following areas:
   • In your home?
   • In your community?
   • In your church?
   • In your workplace?

Notes _____

1. Source unknown.
2. Norman J. Clayton, "My Hope Is in the Lord." © 1945 and 1973, Norman Clayton Publishing Co.

CHAPTER TWO

Overseeing God's People

I. What are elders?

A. Presbuteros

1. Old man—bearded one
2. Leaders in the wilderness
3. Governors of cities
4. Sadducean members of the Sanhedrin
5. Governors of the synagogue
6. Leaders of the Christian churches

B. *Episkopos*

1. To watch over
2. Government administrators
3. Chief officer in restored Jerusalem
4. Watches over Christian community

II. The elders' ordination

A. General qualifications

1. Moral integrity
2. Sexual purity
3. Domestic authority
4. Personality suitability
5. Spiritual quality
6. Doctrinal stability
7. Biblical capability

B. Specific qualifications

1. A steward who loves God's church
2. A student who loves God's Word
3. A shepherd who loves God's people

C. Particular considerations

  1. Elders were appointed by apostles
  2. Elders were always plural
  3. No appointment procedure stipulated
  4. No time limit of elders' function

III. The elders' ordination

A. A church must be well-fed

  1. Careful attention to doctrinal purity
  2. Ensure abundance of teaching and counsel

B. A church must be well-led

  1. Clear sense of direction
  2. By example
  3. Encourage "followship" attitude

C. A church must be well-bred

  1. Protected from heretical influence
  2. Preserved from moral disintegration

Titus 1:6-9

An elder must be blameless, the husband of but one wife, a man whose children believe and are not open to the charge of being wild and disobedient. Since an overseer is entrusted with God's work, he must be blameless—not overbearing, not quick-tempered, not given to drunkenness [much wine], not violent, not pursuing dishonest gain. Rather he must be hospitable, one who loves what is good, who is self-controlled, upright, holy and disciplined. He must hold firmly to the trustworthy message as it has been taught, so that he can encourage others by sound doctrine and refute those who oppose it.

Leadership is largely a catalyst for what happens in a corporate body. Studies done in churches in different parts of the world have found that while many churches approach their ministry in different ways and have different emphases, a church that is vital and virile, and achieving that which it appears God has called it to achieve, has without exception a vital, virile leadership.

I think it's also true to say that where you have a fellowship that is weak on leadership, you have a fellowship that is weak period. Now it doesn't mean that leadership is everything, but leadership is a massive part of the health and well-being, and the effectiveness and efficiency of a fellowship of believers. The leaders Titus was commissioned to identify were called elders.

What Are Elders?

We don't use the term "elder" very much in our everyday vocabulary. But it is a common name in biblical understanding, so, let's be absolutely certain that we understand what Paul is getting at when he talks about the necessity for elders. Even though the word elder is used in verse 6, and overseer in verse 7—your translation may say bishop or some other designation—they all refer to the same people.

The apostle Paul uses two different Greek words, and it is quite clear that he uses them interchangeably. The first word is *presbuteros*. The second word is *episkopos*. These two words, while they are quite different, obviously refer to the same kind of people. So when we talk about "elder," "overseer," "bishop" or whatever English translation you are using, understand that we are talking about these two Greek words, presbuteros and episkopos.

Presbuteros

Now, presbuteros is a word you will find in the Septuagint, the Greek translation of the Old Testament. Some of your Bibles may have in the margin or footnotes the symbol LXX. That is the Roman numeral 70, the symbol for the Septuagint. The original meaning of *presbuteros,* and I love this, is "old man" or "bearded one." My children affectionately call me old man—I hope affectionately—and, of course, I'm to understand that they're using the term very loosely. But, presbuteros originally meant an old man or somebody who had a beard. If you go into many of the societies in the Eastern world today, you'll find that the old men always have beards. And if they are gray beards, they are symbols of dignity and maturity.

The first time I was in Bangladesh and met with a group of Muslim elders I couldn't understand why I was so warmly received. I was told afterwards, it was purely because of my beard. The young missionary who took me there said, "I don't get anything like your reception among those people, even though I've been working among them for years." And he said, "I can't wait until I can grow a beard and see it turn white." The last time I saw him he had started working on his beard, but I'm afraid it was black and resembled five o'clock shadow.

Now then, you'll find that these elders—presbuteros, old men or the bearded ones, as described in the Septuagint—were instrumental in many of the decisions that were made as the people of Israel came out of Egypt and wandered through the wilderness.

Moses is the one who gets all the credit. And he's the one who gets all the blame. Moses is the one who gets all the publicity, but if you read carefully, you'll notice that there were many elders, many mature people, who were responsible for the leadership of the people of Israel. When the children of Israel eventually moved into the Promised Land they ceased to be nomadic and began to establish their towns. Whenever they established a town, they always had a group of elders who were the leaders of the city. And their responsibility was "to sit in the gate." That sounds a little strange to us, but it means that among other things, they fulfilled a judicial function. All the disputes were brought to them. Sitting in the main entrance to the city, these elderly, bearded, mature, dignified people, were the ones who handled the most awkward situations.

Later on in the development of the Jewish people, when the Sanhedrin was founded, there were certain members of the Sanhedrin who were also called the elders. We don't need to go into detail but we do need to be aware that throughout Old Testament and all Jewish experience, there was always the concept of elders. Eventually, after the destruction of Herod's temple and the scattering of the Jewish people throughout the world, if there were 12 Jewish males in any city, they were free to form a synagogue. If they formed a synagogue they had a governor, and the word for governor in the Greek was *presbuteros*.

When Paul, a Jew, along with other Jewish Christians went to the dispersed Jews, preached the gospel and brought them to Christ, they established Christian churches. It's quite understandable that, from that background, they should immediately think in terms of a leadership that was called "elders." And I believe one of the reasons we find the apostle Paul returning to many areas of Asia Minor and establishing the churches and appointing elders is simply because he realized this was a crucial, vital part of the spiritual experience.

Episkopos

Now the word *episkopos* was used commonly by the Greeks in a variety of ways. For instance, in Greek mythology some of the gods were called *episkopoi*. This doesn't mean that the gods were bishops. *Episkopos* means literally to "watch over," "look after" or "care for." So when they gave the title episkopos to one of their gods, the idea was that he was a caring, watching, overseeing god who was particularly concerned for a city, a people, a country.

In the same way, the Greeks had government officials with the title episkopos. For instance, when the Greeks were able to overrun certain areas and subsidiary nations came under their control, they would send administrators to the various cities. The title for the administrator was episkopos. He was the person who was going to oversee. When the people of Israel came back from their captivity and restored Jerusalem, some of the leaders in that particular restoration period and some of the administrators of the rebuilding of Jerusalem were given the same title.

This term, therefore, came quite naturally into use in the new Christian fellowships, because as they were founded, they not only needed a mature, dignified people of experience who could function in leadership roles, but also people who could administrate, oversee, care for and be responsible for this community.

Now, that's a very quick sketch of the background of these two words, presbuteros and episkopos. The question has been asked, Why does the apostle Paul sometimes use presbuteros and other times episkopos? I will suggest just two answers. One is possibly that presbuteros was the word to describe the character of the elder, the idea being that he was the old, bearded one, or to put it more simply, Paul thought in terms of these elders being characterized by maturity and dignity. But episkopos described their function rather than their character.

Another suggestion is that the Hebrew people, probably because of the Septuagint, would be more favorably disposed towards presbuteros, and those of the Greek background would probably understand more clearly the meaning of episkopos. Whatever the case, as Titus is given the job of ordaining elders in these areas, it's rather obvious that Paul, under the inspiration of the Holy Spirit, is saying that these churches need people who are characterized by dignity, maturity and wisdom, and who are going to be seriously involved in overseeing, leading and caring for this fellowship of believers.

The Elders' Ordination

Who are these people to be? I want to suggest, first of all, some general qualifications and then some specific qualities.

General Qualifications

Notice in Titus 1:6,9 that the Apostle maps out some of the general qualifications. (See parallel passage in 1 Tim. 3.) "An elder must be blameless." That doesn't mean he has to be perfect, because it would rather narrow our choices, wouldn't it? "An elder must be blameless, the husband of but one wife, a man whose children believe and are not open to the charge of being wild and disobedient. Since an overseer is entrusted with God's work, he must be blameless—not overbearing, not quick-tempered, not given to much wine, not violent, not pursuing dishonest gain. Rather, he must be hospitable, one who loves what is good, who is self-controlled, upright, holy and disciplined. He must hold firmly to the trustworthy message as it has been taught, so that he can encourage others by sound doctrine and refute those who oppose it."

Now, one of the interesting things about these general qualifications is that they are not all that special. In other words, it seems to me that the general qualifications Paul is outlining here are characteristics that can reasonably be expected of any man who professes to be a follower of Jesus Christ.

I heard about a management seminar in the secular business world in which a debate was going on about the qualifications for managers. One gentleman listening to all the qualifications being spelled out, took out a New Testament, turned to Titus 1 and 1 Timothy 3, and pointed out to the leader of the seminar that they were paying an awful lot of money to hear from him what they could have gotten for nothing from the Bible. The interesting thing about it is that in management today, when they are looking for people who can give leadership, they want those who have basically the qualifications spelled out here in this passage of Scripture. This does not mean that we take lightly these qualifications. What it does mean is that elders are people whose lives show minimally the characteristics of spiritual maturity that can reasonably be expected of those who are serious about the Lord.

First, "An elder must be blameless." The word "blameless" here means a man whose life is characterized by *moral integrity*. In other words, he is firmly committed to Christian, biblical morality. And he is known to be firmly committed to this not only by the stands he takes but by the life-style he exhibits.

The apostle Paul in the parallel passage, points out that this blamelessness, or this beyond-reproach situation, has to be something that is not only recognized by believers, but is recognized and appreciated by nonbelievers too. "He must also have a good reputation with outsiders" (1 Tim. 3:7). In other words, a person who is going to be suitable, minimally, for this kind of leadership in the Christian Church, is a person who, both in the fellowship and in the secular world, is known as a person who clearly exhibits what biblical, spiritual, Christian morality is all about. And it would be utterly unthinkable for anybody to feel that they can be a leader of the Church of Jesus

An elder must be . . .
a man whose life is
characterized by moral
integrity."

Christ, of God's very own people, and not have that kind of life-style.

Second, this elder is to be a person whose life is characterized by *sexual purity*. Now, I may have taken some liberties here, in interpreting Scripture, but I'm going to explain how I arrived at that conclusion. The expression we have in this passage from the *New International Version* is that an elder must be "the husband of but one wife." And you say, How on earth do you get sexual purity from that?

The problem that we have translating this passage is that the Greeks have one word for both man and husband. And they have one word that could be translated either wife or woman. The word that is translated *husband* here is translated "husband" 50 times in the New Testament, but is translated "man" 156 times. By the same token, the word that is translated *wife* here is translated "wife" 92 times, but 129 times as "woman." Therefore, I think a very good case could be made for this expression literally to mean the elder has to be a one-woman man.

Now, there's a rather colloquial twist to that, but it seems to me what the Apostle is saying is that this elder has to be somebody who specifically—within the context of moral integrity—is a man who is known for his sexual purity.

Sexual purity was particularly important in the early Church. Because they were having so many problems with sexual immorality, it was absolutely imperative that they put some distance between the Church and a corrupt and depraved society, particularly in the area of sexuality. I believe this emphasis is necessary today. The Church of Jesus Christ has to put a lot of distance between ourselves and the sexual immorality and impurity that has become normative in our society.

Therefore, while I am not going to make a big case out of this, my suggestion is that this expression, "The husband of but one wife," would probably be better translated "a one-woman man." However, if you want to leave it "The husband of but one wife," then you have to ask, how does this apply?

Some suggest that Paul was prohibiting anyone who was engaging in polygamy from being a leader in the Christian Church. But Christian scholars say that is hardly the point because if they were actually engaging in polygamy, they would not be allowed to function in any capacity in the Church in the first place.

Others see in this statement a reference to divorce and remarriage. And some, including Tertullian, the church father, have gone so far as to say that it could only be a man who had married once, and if his wife had died, he was not to remarry, or his eldership would be taken away.

If the expression is taken purely at face value, it would disqualify single men from eldership. That would mean neither the Lord Himself nor Paul could be elders!

The third general qualification for leadership is *domestic authority*. Paul goes on to say that this elder must be "a man whose children believe and are not open to the charge of being wild and disobedient." In the parallel passage in 1 Timothy, Paul explains why he believes this. And he adds what seems to be an incontrovertible rhetorical question: If a man can't manage his family, how on earth can he manage the Church? This, of course, is a good question.

Now then, we run into a problem right away. What happens when you have an elder whose family is grown and gone? They are no longer his responsibility; he has little impact upon their lives. What about the person who has brought up his kids in a family where he was clearly a spiritual authority and recognized as the head of the family, where he gave his children every opportunity to grow up in the nurture and admonition of the Lord, and to all intents and purposes while they were at home they went along as consistent young believers. But they went wild after they left home. Is that person to be disqualified? That's something that needs to be carefully addressed.

It seems to me that we have to decide how long a father is responsible for his kids? I think one thing ought to be quite clear, and here we'll go to an irreducible minimum again: When we're talking about people who are qualified for eldership, we're talking about people who are clearly exercising spiritual leadership in their families. They are exhibiting leadership that is being accepted by the children. Furthermore, I think we're looking for people who have such a testimony in their family, where it's hardest to have a testimony, that their kids are being won over by the testimony of the old bearded one, the head of the family.

There is no guarantee that our children are going to believe. But, if the father is running that family with no sense of leadership and in such a way that it is a disaster, if he is not demonstrating a winsomeness of spiritual experience, and the net result is that the kids are a mess, then it ought to be rather obvious that this person is not going to be qualified for eldership in the Church of Jesus Christ. This is a serious thing, but I think the apostle Paul is making an awful lot of sense here. If I cannot exhibit in my own family leadership, authority and a winsome Christian testimony, and if I can't have an impact on my own kids, then of course, it is highly unlikely that I could ever be able to have any meaningful leadership, exercise any spiritual authority or make any powerful impact in the Church of Jesus Christ.

Since an overseer is entrusted with God's work, he must have what I call *personality suitability*.

What Paul is saying about this is, there are some people whose lives just aren't under control. They are domineering people; they are people who are violent in outlook, violent in attitude—sometimes they are physically violent, but more often they are verbally violent. They are people who are getting into situations and stirring them up. They are not disciplined as far as wine is concerned; and they are not disciplined as far as their own finances are concerned.

In other words, some of us have to recognize that there are personality quirks that indicate we do not really have control of our lives, our personalities. And if we don't have control of our lives and personalities, then we are not really suited for this kind of leadership. Let me hasten to add at this point that all of us have personality quirks and aberrations, and this is not saying that an elder is a person who does not have *any* quirks. I believe Scripture is saying that when a person's personality quirks, deficiencies and inadequacies mean he is given to swings of mood, irrational behavior and less than adequate control, that person would not be suited for eldership at this time.

Then, fifth, on a positive note, Paul talks about *spiritual quality.* "Rather," he says in verse 8, "he must be hospitable." The Greek word for hospitable means, literally, "love strangers." That means he is a warm, openhearted person whose home is open to people. And this was of crucial importance in the early Church.

You remember that when evangelism took place in the early Church, there weren't motels for the evangelists to stay in, and if there had been, they couldn't have afforded them. There were inns, but they were not suitable, therefore, the hospitality of people was a key factor in evangelism. If people weren't opening up their homes to these traveling evangelists, the evangelists couldn't go and preach. Moreover, there were many people who when they became believers, upon being baptized were ostracized from their families. They had to go somewhere else to live. So hospitality was not only crucial for evangelism, but absolutely necessary for the caring and nurturing of new believers.

Hospitality is important today, if not quite to that extent. But I firmly believe that somebody who is going to exercise an eldership function in the Church of Jesus Christ has to be a person who is open-armed, openhearted and open-homed, because—and here we go into the second part of this—he "loves what is good." Now this phrase is just one word in the Greek language and it can mean a lover of good things or a lover of good people. In other words, this person has a spiritual quality that shows that he has a genuine concern about that which is good, and he has a deep interest in people who are seeking, before God, to be good. If there's a good thing going, he wants to be part of it. If there's a good man around, he wants to identify with him. If there's something good that is happening, he's part of it.

But then he goes on to say that the elder is also "self-controlled, upright, holy and disciplined." Now, I don't propose going into those terms; we're familiar with them all. What Paul is really saying is that this man has to be able to exhibit spiritual quality in these areas.

Then, sixth, this elder has to have *doctrinal stability*. According to verse 9, "He must hold firmly to the trustworthy message as it has been taught." This person who is going to oversee, look after and care for the Church of God, has to be a person who has been around long enough and has been interested deeply enough to really grasp the truth of the Christian gospel. In other words, he's got a pretty good handle on theology and is deeply committed to the truth. Because of that, he is able to stand firm amid all kinds of spiritual and doctrinal confusion.

Now in the early days of the Christian Church when there was a considerable amount of spiritual and doctrinal confusion, it's rather obvious that the leadership had to be able to live above that confusion; to have their feet firmly set on the truth. I want to suggest to you that we're back in that kind of day today. And I think that any church could reasonably expect its leadership to be based in the truth, so that while all confusion rages around and all kinds of different and crazy ideas are being propagated, the people can look to their leadership and see people who are staunchly stable themselves.

Finally, there should be *biblical capability*. Elders should not only be stable in the truth, but also able to "encourage others by sound doctrine and refute those who oppose it." The Word of God should have taken root in his own heart but at the same time, he should be able to handle the Word of God so that when somebody needs encouragement, he can minister the Word to him. And when somebody needs to be rebuked, he can minister the Word to him. And when some error needs to be refuted, he can minister the Word to him. That's the kind of person Paul is talking about.

Specific Qualities

The person who is called to be an elder has to be *a steward who loves God's Church.* You'll notice that the apostle Paul says in verse 7, "an overseer is entrusted with God's work." The word there is *steward.* Steward means the one who manages the affairs of another. I believe that one of the great things we need in a leader is a tremendous sense of privilege. An elder should constantly

The person who is called to be an elder has to be a steward who loves God's Church. "

be asking, Who am I, Lord, that you should have made me a steward of your very own people?

Some people get into leadership in the Christian Church and grumble and gripe about it all the time. They have no place there. To be in leadership, to be given the task of being a steward of God's very own people, is an inestimable privilege. And if we don't regard it as such, we shouldn't be there.

Second, this leader is *a student who loves God's Word.* If he doesn't love God's Word and doesn't study God's Word, he won't be deeply grounded in It himself and will not be able to minister God's Word to others.

I remember an occasion when I was preaching in another church where I was called in front of the deacons—they were deacons, not elders in that church—and I was roundly rebuked for the way I conducted the service that morning. What upset them was that I didn't give an invitation at the end of the service. I told them I would be happy to talk with them about it, and if they would open their Bibles, we would do a Bible study on invitations.

Well, it didn't take long to do a Bible study on invitations because none of them had their Bibles. So I said, "We've dealt with the problem you have. Let's do a Bible study on deacons. Who can tell me where deacons are mentioned in the Bible?" Not one of them knew one reference to deacon in the Bible. They were businessmen; they were traditionalists; they were men who had their own prejudices; but they were biblically illiterate men.

Such people have no place in a position of leadership. I believe an elder should be a steward who loves God's Church and a student who loves God's Word.

Third, an elder must be *a shepherd who loves God's people.* Now, we have already seen that the idea of overseeing and caring for is an integral part of eldership, and the specific expression *shepherding* is used not a few times in Scripture concerning leadership. Paul, in Acts 20:28, speaking to the Ephesian elders tells them that they are to shepherd God's flock. And you remember when the Lord Jesus gave instructions to Peter—who subsequently called himself an elder—Feed my sheep, feed my lambs, shepherd my sheep (see John 21:15-17). In other words, we're thinking of eldership in terms of one who loves God's people and will give of himself to shepherd them; of one who loves God's Word and will give of himself to study it; of one who loves God's Church and will give of himself to manage, administer and genuinely lead it.

Particular Considerations

You will notice, first of all, that *elders were appointed by the apostles*. The Lord Jesus appointed His apostles; they became the foundation of the Church. But then as the Church began to move out of the apostolic era, it was obvious that the apostles would soon be gone. The elders, therefore, would be the next leaders. So the first elders were appointed by the apostles. The Scriptures tell us that Paul and Barnabas revisited churches and appointed elders (see Acts 14:21-23). But then you'll notice a slightly different development in Titus. Here we have an apostolic delegate who appoints elders. The point is that in the Bible, the only way you ever hear of an elder being ordained is by appointment. The elders were appointed initially by the apostles, subsequently by apostolic delegates.

The second thing we need to note is that elders function in the local church *in the plural*. Now some segments of the historic church have developed what the theologians call a monarchical episcopate. That means they have a bishop or an archbishop. This system was apparently developed in early Church history after the apostolic era, but I believe it has no biblical foundation. Elders in Scripture are spoken of in the plural.

We need to note, third, that *no appointment procedure is specifically stipulated* in Scripture. And, fourth, *there is no mention of a time limit of the elders' function.* But, we do need to bear in mind that Paul speaking to the Ephesians, says that it was the Holy Spirit who had appointed them to be elders (see Acts 20:28).

So, however a church decides to go about appointing elders, they better make absolutely certain that they are people who are called by the Holy Spirit for that ministry.

The Elders' Operation

A Church Must Be Well-fed

First, elders are to see that the church is well-fed. They are to pay *careful attention to doctrinal purity* in the teaching and in the ministering of the church. Also, the elder is to *ensure an abundance of teaching and counsel* for the fellowship.

A Church Must Be Well-led

Second, the elders are to see that the church is well-led. They are to have a *clear sense of direction* for the church. They are themselves to be leaders, but Peter tells us they are to lead primarily by *example* (see 1 Pet. 5:3). They are to be clear-thinking people. Through vision and concern they are to think things through, to develop a sense of direction, and by their very life-styles encourage people to move in that direction.

If the Church is to be well-led, the leadership must *encourage a "followship" attitude.* The thing that determines whether or not you are a leader is if anybody is following. Therefore, elders have to generate in the fellowship an attitude of followship. If they can't do it, they're not leading. That means that there have to be the best possible relations between the elders and those they are caring for.

Now, how you develop followship and how you maintain it is something that needs careful examination. If there is ever an erosion of goodwill between the fellowship and the leadership you may as well put up the shutters, because all you're going to do is get yourself into continual fights and arguments, and that must not be. Not only must there be a tremendous sense of seriousness and privilege on the part of the elders, but on the part of the fellowship there has to be an attitude of willingness to acknowledge their leadership and follow their direction.

Paul, in 1 Thessalonians 5:12,13 says, "Now we ask you, brothers, to respect those who work hard among you, who are over you in the Lord and who admonish you. Hold them in the highest regard in love because of their work. Live in peace with each other." And Hebrews 13:17 exhorts you to "Obey your leaders and submit to their authority. They keep watch over you as men who must give an account. Obey them so that their work will be a joy, not a burden, for that would be of no advantage to you."

The Church must be well-led. The Church must be well-fed.

A Church Must Be Well-bred

Finally, the Church must be well-bred. That means we

have to make absolutely certain that the church is *protected from any heretical influence* and *preserved from any moral disintegration*. And that means that discipline has to be exercised. In our Elmbrook Church constitution we have a statement to the effect that people can be removed from membership if their doctrinal stance is no longer compatible with the church's position, or if their life-style is such that it is not compatible with what we stand for.

Now, who handles that? It has to be handled by the elders. The people who are given the responsibility to lead, oversee and care for the church ought to be able to smell a heretic a mile away. And they don't just turn a blind eye to him. They deal with him and pray at the same time. They recognize the necessity for caring both for the church and for the individual. And if the church is being dragged into the gutter by the immoral behavior of someone in that church, the elders have to deal with it.

Let me remind you that one of the greatest needs in the contemporary Church is leadership that willingly bears the burden, genuinely loves the Church, wholeheartedly serves the Lord and constantly encourages the people. Blessed indeed is the church where such leaders are found.

Questions for further study _____

1. How important is leadership in a body of believers?
2. What are the *general* qualifications listed for the position of elders in the Church? Our author states these general qualifications suggested by the apostle Paul can be reasonably expected of anyone who professes to be a follower of Jesus Christ. How do you feel about this statement?

3. What are the *specific* qualifications listed for elders? Again, how do these qualifications apply to individual believers?

4. Does the "followship" attitude prevail in your church? If you answered yes, what part can you play in seeing that this kind of attitude continues? If you answered no, what steps could you take to help the relationship between the church fellowship and leadership improve?

CHAPTER THREE

Protecting God's People

I. The sound doctrine of the apostles

   A. Sound doctrine is revealed

      1. Not man-made
      2. God-given

   B. Sound doctrine is relayed

   C. Sound doctrine is received

   D. Sound doctrine is reflected

      1. Sound doctrine is healthy
      2. Sound doctrine is health-giving

II. The spurious teaching of the gainsayers

   A. The contentiousness of the spurious teachers

      1. Their reaction was rejection
      2. Their activities were rebellion
      3. Their motives were reprehensible
      4. Their position was refuted

   B. The content of the spurious teaching

      1. Influenced by secular thinking
      2. Involved in syncretic manipulations
      3. Interested in speculative fancies
      4. Included sensual behavior

   C. The consequences of spurious teaching

      1. Faith was destroyed
      2. Households were disrupted
      3. People were trapped

III. The serious responsibility of the elders

A. Deal with the opposition

   1. Rebuke them sharply
   2. Silence them immediately
   3. Teach them patiently

B. Deal with the believers

   1. Protect them from harm
   2. Encourage them in growth
   3. Help them develop discernment

Titus 1:10-16

For there are many rebellious people, mere talkers and deceivers, especially those of the circumcision group. They must be silenced, because they are ruining whole households by teaching things they ought not to teach—and that for the sake of dishonest gain. Even one of their own prophets has said, "Cretans are always liars, evil brutes, lazy gluttons." This testimony is true. Therefore, rebuke them sharply so that they will be sound in the faith and will pay no attention to Jewish myths or to the commands of those who reject the truth. To the pure, all things are pure, but to those who are corrupted and do not believe, nothing is pure. In fact, both their minds and consciences are corrupted. They claim to know God, but by their actions they deny Him. They are detestable, disobedient and unfit for doing anything good.

The apostle Paul has told Timothy, one of his young associates, to stay on in Crete. Individuals had come to Christ, and now they were being encouraged to form themselves into communities of believers called churches. The main task Titus has been given is to put things in order in those churches, including the appointing of elders to oversee and to care for the well-being of the church.

We have noticed, however, that there is a much

deeper, greater and grander thing going on while Titus is humanly bringing together the details of these fellowships. And it is simply this: God Himself is in Crete at that particular time, purifying for Himself a people who are His very own, eager to do what is good.

The theme of Titus is simply this: On the human level, these men are responsible for bringing into order the life and affairs of the local church. But on the other level, while they are doing that, God is at work producing in that church a people who are His very own, who are going to be clearly identifiable, clearly distinguishable, utterly distinctive as a very special people, uniquely God's people in that area.

Whenever, therefore, we talk about the church, we may talk about organizational structure; we may talk about institutionalized factors; we may talk about church government; we may talk about constitution or whatever else may be necessary; but we must always remember that at the end of all these things must be the purifying of a people for God Himself, God's very own people. With this in mind I want to show you the importance of protecting God's people.

It is rather obvious that the letter Paul is writing to Titus at this particular time uses pretty tough language. He quotes a very uncomplimentary comment one of the Cretans made about people living in Crete. Then he says that the poet is absolutely right! Paul's concern, of course, is that along with all the infant churches being founded in different parts of the Middle East, these people in Crete are struggling; they have much opposition. There are many difficulties, not only in opposition to them as individual believers, but also in founding the churches. These new Christians are having a difficult time coming together and seeing themselves as God's very own people.

The apostle Paul says that one of the great responsibilities of the leadership of those churches is, among other things, to protect God's people and the fellowship of believers so they might in actuality be God's very own people.

The Sound Doctrine of the Apostles

In verse 9, something we touched on in the last chapter, Paul says that the responsibility of the elders, among many other things, is that they "encourage others by sound doctrine and refute those who oppose it." In other words, the emphasis is on sound doctrine. Paul says that the leadership of the church must be deeply committed to sound doctrine, making it constantly and abundantly available to the people for two reasons. First, for the nurturing and the encouraging of those who are believers; and second, for the refuting of those who are in opposition.

Now he moves into an elaboration of what he means concerning the refuting of those who oppose individual believers and the establishing of local churches. The emphasis is still on sound doctrine. You'll find the expression recurring frequently in the pastoral Epistles—the two Epistles to Timothy and this Epistle to Titus.

Sound Doctrine Is Revealed

Paul is very insistent that the sound doctrine delivered to him and to the other apostles *is not man-made.* He says quite categorically in Galatians 1:11, "I want you to know, brothers, that the gospel I preached is not something that man made up. I did not receive it from any man, nor was I taught it; rather, I received it by revelation from Jesus Christ."

The Church of Jesus Christ must constantly be reminded that fundamental to the church's life is the sound doctrine, the gospel of our Lord Jesus Christ, that was not made up by man, but was revealed by God.

It is a *God-given* revelation. This is what sets the church apart from the rest of society and is the fundamental difference between a Christian and a non-Christian. Society does not operate on the basis of God's revelations. It operates on the basis of human speculation. A Christian is tuned in to sound doctrine, to divine revelation. A non-Christian couldn't care less about it. He does whatever he feels he should do or he does whatever his society allows him to do. Therefore, one of the fundamental distinctives of the individual Christian and the church is the high regard in which sound doctrine is held, because it comes from divine revelation.

Sound Doctrine Is Relayed

The Apostle goes on to point out that sound doctrine is not only revealed by God, but it must be relayed by those to whom it was being revealed. He has not spoken that which he thought of himself, but he has delivered—and here is one of his favorite expressions—what he first received. "For what I received I passed on to you as of first importance" (1 Cor. 15:3). You remember he introduced his teaching on the communion service in that way (see 1 Cor. 11:23).

So the Apostle says that the churches are founded, because first, God has revealed sound doctrine and, second, the apostles have relayed sound doctrine. But in the third step, in the establishing of individual Christian lives and corporate Christian groups or churches, this sound doctrine is received.

Sound Doctrine Is Received

Writing to the Corinthians, Paul has a similar statement to make: "Now, brothers, I want to remind you of the gospel I preached to you, which you received and on which you have taken your stand. By this gospel you are saved, if you hold firmly to the word I preached to you. Otherwise, you have believed in vain. For what I received I passed on to you" (15:1-3). Do you see the picture? Sound doctrine is revealed; sound doctrine is relayed; sound doctrine is received. It is received by those who hear; they believe and—the Apostle puts it very graphically—they take their stand upon it.

What then is the basis of the individual Christian life? What then is the basis of the community of believers in the church? It is the basis of sound doctrine. Sound doctrine that has been revealed; sound doctrine that has been relayed; sound doctrine that has been received by people who believe it and unequivocally take their stand upon it.

Sound Doctrine Is Reflected

But then, sound doctrine must be reflected. And I want to point this out by drawing your attention to the word "sound" that Paul uses here. In the Greek it is the word from which we get our English word "hygiene" or "hygienic." It literally means "sound" or "healthy" or "well." In fact, on occasions it was used as a greeting in the Middle East in the time of the apostle Paul.

I was rather pleased to learn this because I remember years ago, in England, we had two American students in our Bible School. They were engaged and they used to greet each other rather warmly every morning, much to the delight of the other students. He was called Gene, which was kind of strange to English ears anyway because that's a woman's name in England; and she was called Ena. And their greeting always went like this: "Hi, Gene." "Hi, Ena." But we could never quite understand what hyenas and hygiene had to do with each other.

But I discovered that their greeting was valid. Hygiene, which is also the Greek word here, is a greeting.

The point of it is, however, that when the Apostle says that sound doctrine is the key, what he is really saying is this: The preaching which is being revealed, relayed and received, must be reflected, because sound doctrine is healthy, and sound doctrine that is healthy is always health-giving. So if you want to find a healthy Christian, look for a Christian who is plugged into healthy teaching. If you want to find a healthy church, look for a church that is built upon healthy teaching. Both sound teaching and healthy doctrine produce health-giving living. When sound doctrine is imparted to individuals and to corporate groups of people, there will be evidence of vitality, health and spiritual virility.

Why is it that individual Christians sometimes seem to be spiritually anemic? The answer quite simply is that they are deficient in sound, healthy teaching. Why do some churches seem to be withering on the vine? More often than not, it's because inadequate attention is being given to sound, health-giving, health-promoting teaching.

The apostle Paul, therefore, insists that the responsibility of Titus and the elders he appoints is to safeguard the propagation of *healthy* and *health-giving teaching*. If you're going to have healthy saints, you need sound doctrine. If you're going to have a healthy church, you've got to have sound doctrine.

It might be appropriate at this juncture to draw atten-

If you want to find a healthy Christian, look for a Christian who is plugged into healthy teaching."

tion to another favorite Pauline expression—this is a faithful saying! A study of the many passages containing this phrase can prove most beneficial in identifying what Paul classified as "sound doctrine."

The Spurious Teaching of the Gainsayers

Now then, in total contrast to the sound doctrine and teaching of the apostles, Paul tells Titus that there is an awful lot of spurious teaching coming from the opposers, or more literally, the contradictors. Now, if you remember your Latin, *contradict* means "to speak against." And the Greek word used here is the exact parallel. In other words, there were in the community of believers and surrounding the community of believers those who were flatly contradicting sound teaching. They were opposers, contradictors, speakers against. And what they were producing was utterly spurious.

The Apostle talks to Titus about it and says, "Your responsibility, Titus, in that fellowship, and the responsibility of those elders who will be appointed, is to make sure you handle these spurious teachers and their spurious teaching correctly."

The Contentiousness of the Spurious Teachers

First of all, let's take a look at the contentiousness of these spurious teachers. Their reaction to the gospel the apostle Paul and Titus had taught to Crete was utter *rejection*. They are described at the end of verse 14 as "those who reject the truth."

Now, let's face it. Whenever you present the gospel to someone, he has the freedom to accept or reject what is being said. We are not responsible for people's response to or reaction against sound teaching. But we are responsible to see that they have the sound teaching, so they can either respond to it or reject it.

Always remember that in the propagation of the truth that was revealed by the Lord to His apostles and through them to the Church, there will always be rejectors. There will always be those who don't want to do it God's way. But here's the ironic thing: That does not necessarily mean that they want to divorce themselves from God's people. In fact, frequently you'll find that those who are resistant to what God says want to derive considerable benefit from God's people. And frequently you'll find there are people who are living in blatant rejection of the truth who still insist they have as much right to be God's people as those who accept the truth.

Now, we have to understand that those kinds of people in the community of believers have total freedom to reject the truth communicated to them, but they do not have total freedom to go on propagating their rejection within the church.

It's rather interesting to notice that the Apostle not only outlines their reaction, he actually says, second, the sum total of their activities is *rebellion*. Their reaction is rejection; their activities can simply be characterized as rebellious activities. Verse 10 says that they are "rebellious people, mere talkers," deceiving all kinds of people. He says that you will find in the Christian community, and surrounding the Christian community, those who reject the truth. But for reasons known only to themselves they still stick around God's people; they are rebellious in their life-style; they reject the truth committed to them; they do an awful lot of talking; they are forever propagating what they believe. And the end product is that they are deceiving all kinds of people; they are leading them astray. "Titus," says Paul, "watch them. Don't allow these people to go around spreading their ideas; don't allow them to go around affecting and infecting God's very own people. See them for what they are. They are truth rejectors and they are fundamentally rebellious against God."

Then he goes on to point out something else. He says not only something about their reactions to the truth and their activities among God's people, but he also has something very strong to say about their motives. Third, he said their motives are utterly *reprehensible,* that underlying all their activity is "dishonest gain." Financial considerations are underneath all they are doing.

Let's broaden that just a little and suggest that it is not uncommon to find people who reject the truth, who are rebellious in their life-style, yet still demand and insist on having a place among the community of believers. They go on propagating their rebellion, insisting on their rejection, confusing and deceiving all kinds of people because they're getting benefit out of it for themselves. Not necessarily financial gain, maybe they're getting a hearing. Maybe they're getting some attention. Maybe Christians are the only people who listen to them. Maybe it's the only chance they have of getting a crowd of people to even show any interest in them whatsoever.

Fourth, Paul says to Titus, "Titus, make sure that their positions are *refuted.*" "Therefore, rebuke them sharply" (v. 13). Now, there is a feeling in society at large and in the Christian community in particular, that if you refute anybody, you're cutting them down; you're rejecting them. All too frequently this is characterized as non-Christian. Have you heard that?

I want to tell you something. If you allow those who reject the gospel of Christ to go on propagating their rejection and flaunting their rebellion, and allow them to confuse and deceive God's people, you're acting non-Christian if you let them get away with it. It is not non-Christian to sharply rebuke those who are in error, far from it. It is non-Christian to simply shrug your shoulders and just assume it will go away or it doesn't matter or, even worse, to adopt the pseudo-benevolent pastor who proclaims, "Well, everybody's entitled to his own opinion."

But everybody is not entitled to propagate spurious opinions in the community of believers. And it's the responsibility of the leadership to see what is being said by whom and if there is spurious preaching. It is the responsibility of the leadership to rebuke it. Sharply.

The Content of the Spurious Teaching

What was it these people in Crete were saying that was so wrong, and which Paul was so concerned about? We don't have a clear statement of what it was that was so wrong, but there are numerous clues in the letters to Timothy and this Epistle to Titus that we can put together and perhaps come up with—let's call them educated guesses—as to what the specific nature of this spurious teaching was.

We know this spurious teaching was fundamentally *influenced by secular thinking.* For instance, in 1 Timothy 4:3, speaking of these teachers Paul said: "They forbid people to marry and order them to abstain from certain foods." His answer to that is, "God created [these things] to be received with thanksgiving by those who believe and who know the truth." There you have a major difference between what the spurious teachers were teaching and what the Word of God teaches.

The Word of God teaches that God has given us these things richly to enjoy, but these teachers were saying that

there are certain things you must not touch and not eat.
Now the tendencies were toward what we might call
ascetic emphases. Their approach was this: There is
something fundamentally wrong with matter; there is
something fundamentally evil about the body; therefore,
we have to rigidly watch this body and be very careful how
we handle material things. And you become spiritual, they
would say, by rigid and determined denial and discipline of
the physical body and its God-given desires and needs,
thus allowing the liberation of your spirit to take place.
Now, that's one clue to what they were teaching.

First Timothy 6:20 gives us another clue in this
regard. "Timothy, guard what has been entrusted to your
care. Turn away from godless chatter and the opposing
ideas of what is falsely called knowledge." These people
who had ascetic emphases were also people who claimed
to have special knowledge. Now, the Greek word for
"knowledge" in this sense is *gnosis*. Those who began to
develop certain ideas became known as *gnostics*.

Gnostics had an approach to life that was in diametric
opposition to what the Scriptures teach. Gnostics believed
that God and spiritual things were totally separate from
the world and material things. Gnosticism claims that God
and things spiritual are essentially good; but the world and
things material are fundamentally evil. This is called *dual-
ism*. They did not believe that things came from one common source and that God was the beginning of all things.
They believed that there were two sources; that which
was good and that which was evil.

They believed that to be able to handle evil things you
had to be able to handle the material. But they also
believed that you needed special insight—special *gnosis,*
special experience, special knowledge. And they believed
they had it. They believed furthermore that if you didn't

belong to their group you didn't have it. So what was the result? They became very supercilious: They suffered from a superiority complex. These people, rigid in their beliefs, believed they had a special "in" on the truth that was very carefully refined, which put them in a category far beyond and above everybody else. They felt totally superior. They demonstrated their superiority by utterly scorning the moral principles that were being taught in the Church of Jesus Christ. They said these moral principles were either from the cosmos—which was evil and designed to bring us into slavery to it—or they were simply man-made ideas.

To show their utter scorn, Gnostics refused to adhere to the moral principles of the Scriptures. Sometimes for ascetic reasons; sometimes they were just plain licentious. And they acted openly; they didn't care; they did their own thing, because they had an "in" on the truth.

Now this was one of the powerful influences coming into the church. And, Paul said in 2 Timothy 2:17, "Their teaching will spread like gangrene." That's complimentary, isn't it? "Among them are Hymenaeus and Philetus, who have wandered away from the truth." Paul goes on to tell what the gnostics were teaching: "They say that the resurrection has already taken place, and [accordingly] they destroy the faith of some" (vv. 17-18).

To say the Resurrection had already taken place meant the only resurrection that would ever be was when Christ rose again from the dead. Gnostics maintained that for believers to believe they will have a part in the Resurrection is total error. Not only is it total error, they said, it is utterly abhorrent to think that the body, which is so evil, will ever be raised up; God is not going to make anything good out of that.

In teaching this idea they were denying the great hope

The great hope of the believer is that one day we will be raised with Christ and will share eternal glory with Him."

of the believer, which is that one day we will be raised with Christ and will share eternal glory with Him. This influence—which we will call for want of a better term a "gnostic" influence—that was coming into the church was purely secular. It had nothing to do with biblical revelation. In fact, more often than not, it flew totally in the face of biblical revelation.

Yet gnostics reserved the right to breeze into the church with their secular thoughts and their secular teaching and confuse all manner of people.

Now, it's the easiest thing in the world for people to become totally secularized in their thinking. Then they bring their thinking into the community of believers, demonstrating their utter biblical illiteracy, but chattering on about secular concepts and ideas, trying to twist them into biblical or spiritual principles. The secular world does not take time to find out what God's Word says, but they bring all their secular thinking to bear on the affairs of the church and try to fit the church into the mold of basic secular thinking. When people do that, the apostle Paul says, "Rebuke them sharply."

The second thing we can note about the content of this spurious teaching is that it was involved in *syncretic manipulations*. By that I mean they were not only bringing in gnostic influences, they were bringing in all kinds of Jewish influences and uniquely Christian ideas as well. And they were trying to form a syncretism of all three. Does that sound familiar?

For instance, they loved some aspects of what the gnostics were teaching, but they were really quite excited about many of the Jewish traditions, particularly what the apostle Paul calls: all kinds of genealogies and fanciful ideas (see 1 Tim. 1:4; Titus 3:9). These ideas fit in nicely with the way they were going. They even found some aspects of apostolic Christian teaching very interesting as well. So they pulled the whole bunch together and tried to make it all fit, then taught it in the church.

Now, I don't know if you've ever noticed this, but there is a great move in our society today to be delightfully and totally tolerant of what everybody believes and thinks. Often this is a commendable attitude, but very often we finish up with our tolerance producing total chaos. Particularly in the community of believers we try to bring in totally incompatible ideas—some from here, some from there, some from somewhere else—mold them together and come up with a wonderful solution.

Let me give you one simple illustration. Do you remember TM, transcendental meditation? Do you remember how that was the big fad and how all kinds of believers got excited about it? They knew they were supposed to meditate, so they brought in Christian concepts of meditation, and quoted things like "Wait upon the Lord."

Believers didn't like it, however, when it was pointed out that transcendental meditation is nothing more than Hinduism, dressed up to confuse people. They refuted it, rejected it and detested it when they were told; but it was true nevertheless. And you would find, not infrequently, believers who were into TM. They were saying that it was really helping their spiritual growth. Now, how Hinduism can help a Christian to grow beats me, because it is a principle in total opposition to all that Christianity stands for. But this is the kind of thing that still goes on in the Christian church—syncretic manipulations.

So, in Crete, teaching was based on secular thought while trying to come up with a syncretic amalgam of Jewish and Greek, and uniquely Christian ideas. They were going to be very tolerant and accept it all and finish up with a delightful mishmash, which sounds great, but is an utter insult to the basic principle that our truth is what God has revealed through the apostles and has preserved for us in His Word.

Third, their spurious teaching was *interested in all kinds of speculative fancies.* The apostle Paul points out in Titus 1:14 that they were all excited about Jewish myths. And in 1 Timothy 1:4, he talks about these same myths and endless genealogies.

Some of the Jewish teachers felt there were gaps in the information made available to them in Scripture. So they set to work with great gusto and ingenuity filling in these gaps with the most dramatic and fantastic, in the real sense of the word, details. The result was the most unbelievable speculative fancies imaginable. Today it is not uncommon for people to bring into the Christian community things that have the most tenuous relation to biblical truth; they are perhaps 1 percent biblical truth and 99 percent unbelievably fanciful speculation.

Now, it's the easiest thing in the world for something like that to happen. Paul tells Titus to watch these guys. Because if he's not careful he'll have a church full of people who are off into the most crazy, faddish, speculative hunches imaginable, assuming it to be good, sound, solid Christianity. Watch them, he said.

Then he also points out that their teaching *included much sensual behavior.* In Titus 1:16 Paul said that these people who are engaging in this kind of teaching "claim to know God." That is probably another passing reference to the gnosis idea. "They claim to know God, but by their actions they deny Him. They are detestable, disobedient and unfit for doing anything good."

In case you need a commentary as to what Paul means specifically, read 2 Timothy 3:1-5: "There will be terrible times in the last days. People will be lovers of themselves, lovers of money, boastful, proud, abusive, disobedient to their parents, ungrateful, unholy, without love, unforgiving, slanderous, without self-control, brutal, not lovers of the good, treacherous, rash, conceited, lovers of pleasure rather than lovers of God—having a form of godliness but denying its power." Having a form of godliness, or as he says in Titus, "They claim to know God." But, by what they do, they deny that very claim.

Then see what he says—and please, ladies, I didn't say this, Paul did. "They are the kind who worm their way into homes and gain control over weak-willed women, who are loaded down with sins and are swayed by all kinds of evil desires, always learning but never able to acknowledge the truth" (2 Tim. 3:6-7). Now Paul isn't saying that all women are weak-willed. What he is saying is that some of them are; they're just like men in that regard. Weak-willed women are very susceptible to people who, in the name of spirituality, are actually engaging in all manner of sensuality.

Let's face it. Women who have been hurt, who are very lonely, who are having a hard time and are looking for some affection, are easy pickings for these kinds of people. Not infrequently, in our singles ministry, we have discovered people making loud protestations of spirituality when it became abundantly clear to us that all they were interested in was rank sensuality, and some of the Bible study was taking place in bed. "Rebuke them sharply," says the Apostle.

Let's take it a little bit further. It is not uncommon in today's churches to find people who carry big Bibles; and alongside the big Bibles and the Bible studies is a life-style characterized by rank sensuality and utter sexual immorality. "Rebuke them sharply," says the Apostle.

The Consequences of Spurious Teaching

Paul's concern about this spurious teaching—as was the case with Hymenaeus and Philetus—is that their *faith was destroyed.* In another place he says that shipwreck was made of their faith (see 1 Tim. 1:19). In yet another he says that whole *households have been turned upside down.* What is really happening in all this is that *people are falling into the trap of the devil* and are being taken captive by him to do his will. In other words, the Church of Jesus Christ had better recognize that alongside sound doctrine, holy teaching, there is always the possibility that some people who reject the truth, who have rebellious life-styles, are identifying with God's people and with endless chatter are propagating their totally nonbiblical views.

The net result of this will be that their teaching, chattering and life-styles will destroy the faith of some, make utter shipwreck of the faith of others, totally disrupt some households and will result in some people being utterly captivated by the devil himself, so that they fall into unbelievable sin. And that's what Paul is warning Titus about. "You had better make sure you have some good leadership in that church, Titus, because this is the kind of junk that's going on. This is the kind of stuff that needs to be handled."

The Serious Responsibility of the Elders

Deal with the Opposition

The serious responsibility of the elders in all of this is, first of all, to deal with the opposition—the gainsayers, the contradictors, these fellows or women, whoever they are, who are doing this damage.

First, *rebuke them sharply.* Everybody is going to say you're non-Christian; they're going to say you're putting them down; they're going to say you're cutting them off at their stocking tops. Let them say it. Do what the Bible tells you to do. Rebuke them sharply.

Second, *silence them immediately.* As soon as you find out what they're doing make absolutely certain that they are silenced immediately. And the word Paul uses for silence here means literally to put a muzzle on them. He says to the leadership of the church, get to this situation and rebuke these people and take them out of positions where they have the opportunity of propagating that which is in opposition to the Christian gospel.

If that sounds harsh, let me point out the third thing he says in addition to rebuking them sharply and silencing them immediately: *Teach them patiently.* Notice what he says in 2 Timothy 2:25. He says the servant of the Lord "must gently instruct, in the hope that God will grant them repentance leading them to a knowledge of the truth."

Now, you have to rebuke them to point out the error of what they are saying. You have to silence them to protect those who are affected by what they are saying. But it doesn't mean you kick them out and say, get out of here and get lost. By no means. Rebuke them, silence them and then take every opportunity to patiently teach them, in hopes they might come to a knowledge of the truth.

Deal with the Believers

Then there's a responsibility to deal with the believers.

First, the responsibility to *protect them from harm;* second, a constant responsibility to *encourage them in growth;* third, a constant responsibility to *help the believers develop discernment.*

I started out my working career as a banker when I was 17 years of age, and nobody in the bank ever taught me how to recognize a counterfeit note. One day I said to one of the senior men, "Why doesn't somebody tell me how to recognize a counterfeit note?"

He said, "Oh, we never do that. We just give you lots of real ones to count. You'll get so used to counting the real ones that if you come across a counterfeit you will know it."

I have no doubt that it is helpful for some people to study false teaching in order to recognize false teachers and false followers, but it is most important that we become deeply familiar with the truth. Not infrequently I have been surprised at the speed with which relatively new believers become aware of teaching that does not sound quite right. Not because they have taken advanced courses in heresies but because their hearts and minds are becoming attuned and accustomed to the truth in all its beauty.

Questions for further study _____

1. What reasons are given in this chapter for the importance of protecting God's people?
2. The sound doctrine of the apostles is first revealed, then relayed, received and reflected. How is sound doctrine revealed? Who is to relay sound doctrine? Who receives sound doctrine? What distinguishes whether or not sound doctrine is reflected?
3. Those in Paul's day who opposed the sound doctrine of the apostles were said to show rejection, rebellion, reprehensible motives. Who or what group can you name who today are "rebellious people, mere talkers,"

deceiving all kinds of people? According to the apostle Paul, how are believers to handle rebellious people?

4. Compare some of the teaching that was around in Paul's day with the teaching of God's Word. What kinds of "spurious" teaching is around today?

CHAPTER FOUR

Training
God's People

I. The intent of the training

    A. To explain what is sound

    B. To emphasize what is suitable

    C. To encourage what is strategic

    D. To engage what is skeptical

II. The extent of the training

    A. Managing the people
   1. Male and female
   2. Young and old
   3. Deprived and advantaged

    B. Mobilizing the team
   1. Appointing elders
   2. Motivating the older women

    C. Modeling the truth
   1. Life-style that shows consistency
   2. Communication that shows conviction

    D. Maintaining the pressure
   1. Proper application
   2. Correct authority
   3. Necessary assertiveness

III. The Content of the training

    A. The older men

    B. The older women

    C. The younger women

    D. The younger men

    E. The disadvantaged

Titus 2:1-10

You must teach what is in accord with sound doctrine. Teach the older men to be temperate, worthy of respect, self-controlled, and sound in faith, in love and in endurance. Likewise, teach the older women to be reverent in the way they live, not to be slanderers or addicted to much wine, but to teach what is good. Then they can train the younger women to love their husbands and children, to be self-controlled and pure, to be busy at home, to be kind, and to be subject to their husbands, so that no one will malign the word of God. Similarly, encourage the young men to be self-controlled. In everything set them an example by doing what is good. In your teaching show integrity, seriousness and soundness of speech that cannot be condemned, so that those who oppose you may be ashamed because they have nothing bad to say about us. Teach slaves to be subject to their masters in everything, to try to please them, not to talk back to them, and not to steal from them, but show that they can be fully trusted, so that in every way they will make the teaching about God our Saviour attractive.

The apostle Paul, along with Titus, had ministered in Crete in an area that was totally ignorant of the truth. They had preached the gospel and invited the Cretans to come into a personal relationship with the living will of

Jesus. Then Paul had to move on, but he left Titus there and said, "All right, now take them on from here, Titus."

It's one thing, of course, to lead people to a personal relationship with Christ. This is fundamental; this is basic; this is what we do in evangelism. But we are never given the mandate to leave them there. We are to disciple people in the arena of fellowship of believers in the Church of Jesus Christ. And so, Titus was given a big task. Paul spelled it out as going to each of the towns on Crete and organizing the believers, appointing elders who would oversee their spiritual life and ministry and well-being. In other words, establishing churches.

But Paul is careful to point out to Titus that what is really going on while Titus does that is that God is purifying for Himself a people who are His very own, and this is what's unique about the Church of Jesus Christ.

The Church—on one hand an invisible, mystical, universal body, but on the other hand, a local, tangible, visible body of believers—is actually God's very own people. And, it is important not only that Christians individually know how to behave as those who have a personal relationship with Christ, it's very important that Christians collectively, as a body of believers, know how to behave, so they can model how people and communities are to be together.

So the task the apostle Paul gives Titus is a monumental task. It is the task of appointing elders who will be able to lead and direct and oversee and encourage and preach to a group of people so that they can be, in a very real sense, known as the people of God in that particular vicinity.

We have studied what the Apostle told Titus in the first chapter of his Epistle, and we've noticed that the emphasis all along is on sound teaching, sound doctrine. That expression occurs also in the other two pastoral Epistles, Paul's letters to Timothy. It is obvious that Paul is reminding these young co-workers that fundamental to all spiritual experience is the teaching of the Word of God. The word for sound in the Greek, as we've pointed out, is the word from which we get hygiene; and it means literally, "healthy," healthy teaching.

Of course, the reason Paul is emphasizing the necessity for healthy teaching is that the pagan areas in which these people are living are infested with ideas, philosophies and doctrines that are decidedly unhealthy. And so in the midst of this unhealthy area Titus is to insist on healthy teaching, truth from the heart of God, applied in such a way that it will produce healthy living in both individuals and the group as a whole.

Titus is also to be sure that the unhealthy teaching is being countered. For the people of God, God's very own people, have to be cared for. There has to be a proper overseeing of them. There has to be correct teaching for them. They have to be protected from things that would hinder, spoil and mar their experience.

Now, in the second chapter of Titus we see that Paul is giving some relatively minute details concerning the training of God's people. As we read through this passage of Scripture, we notice immediately that he divides the congregation into different groups. He talks about older men, older women; he talks about younger women, younger men; and he talks about disadvantaged people like the slaves of that time.

The emphasis, as he divides this congregation into different groups, is on training them. That, of course, is the responsibility of those who have the oversight of a fellowship of believers. They must make the teaching available. I often tell people in ministry, particularly when they get discouraged: "You can take the horse to the water, but you can't make it drink." The responsibility of the elders, the leaders of the Church, is not to make people drink. It is not to make them attend meetings. It is not to make them listen. It is not to make them feed. We can't do that. Many leave the ministry because they feel their responsibility is to make people do what it is patently obvious they are not interested in doing.

One of the greatest releases church leaders ever discover is that it is not their responsibility to make people learn. Their responsibility is to take the horses to the water, but not to feel they have to make them drink. But one thing I've learned is that they do have to make sure there's plenty of water available—plenty of teaching available; but an added incentive is that they should put plenty of salt in the oats. Keep the teaching available, so if there's any degree of life or interest in the people at all, they will want to be part of it.

So, if you find yourself basically interested in the opportunities for spiritual training, understand this: It is not the leaders' responsibility that you are interested. It is not their responsibility that you are doing nothing about it. Their responsibility is to make plenty of water available, and put plenty of salt in your oats; and if you're not drinking after that, frankly, you've got a problem. If you have no appetite for sound teaching, no interest in really discovering the things of God, then you are either spiritually dead or spiritually sick.

Having made the teaching available, it is then necessary for those who have been taught to know how to apply this teaching. And this is basically what Paul talks to Titus about in this passage.

The Intent of the Training

To Explain What Is Sound

First of all, the intent of all spiritual training is to explain what is sound or what is healthy as opposed to what is unhealthy. Or, to put it another way, the intent of all spiritual teaching is to allow people to differentiate between that which is truth and that which is error.

There is considerable confusion in all societies at this time about what is true and what is false. There is considerable confusion concerning that which is revelation of God and that which is speculation of man. And the responsibility that rests upon those who oversee the church is to make sure people have every opportunity to understand the difference between sound and unsound, healthy and unhealthy teaching. That they know the difference between that which comes from God and that which is manufactured by man. And that doesn't happen overnight. It's a long process. It is something to which we give ourselves constantly. And I would have to testify to you quite frankly that the more I personally study the Word of God, the more horrified I am at my ignorance of what it says.

I received a letter from England asking me to do the Bible teaching for 16,000 young people who would be gathering over there one summer. They asked me to teach a series of messages based on the prophet Isaiah. And the funny thing about it is that I had never in over 35 years of preaching, preached a series on the prophet Isaiah. I thought, Wow, if I take that on, I'm really going to have to get down to it; I've been preaching 35 years and yet there are great big holes in my knowledge of areas of the Word of God.

I think we all need to be aware of the big holes in our

knowledge of the Word of God and our understanding of the things of God. That is why it is so important that the teaching and training of the Church of Jesus Christ be taken seriously so that we understand sound teaching. I am deeply alarmed at people who show little interest or involvement in sound teaching.

To Emphasize What Is Suitable

I want you to notice an interesting little expression in Titus 2:1. "You," said the apostle to Titus, "must teach what is in accord with sound doctrine." The older versions of the Bible use a lovely old word: "That which is *becoming* sound doctrine."

What he is saying is, "You are to teach people that when they've got the doctrine straight in their heads, they then need to know what kind of behavior is becoming that sound teaching."

Let me give you an illustration. I've heard that there are some patterns and fabrics that are not very becoming to people who have certain body shapes. For example, some people should not wear fabrics with stripes that run in a particular direction, or unfortunately, those stripes will accentuate what does not need accentuating at all. If you wear stripes that go the other way, they sort of help. I don't understand how it works; I'm not even sure if it's true. But the word that is used to describe wearing that which is suitable is "becoming." You are wearing a very becoming dress. That hat is very becoming to you. It's an old English word and it's a nice word.

While I was thinking about this, for some reason, I thought about that strange, silly man, Woody Allen. Woody Allen, whose problems are well-known—he's made a living out of advertising them—was given the privilege of accompanying President Ford's wife Betty to a certain gala event in New York City. You may remember that Betty Ford showed up dressed as a first lady should for such an event; but Allen showed up in a tux and tennis shoes. Most unbecoming. He was doing things that were just not suited to the occasion; he was wearing things that were grotesquely out of order.

Now, the word "becoming" means you are doing things that are suitable; things that are in accord with; things that are not grotesquely out of sync with what is happening.

Paul's point to Titus is this: When you have taught the people sound teaching, train them to behave in a way that is becoming, that is suitable to the teaching you have taught them.

There is in all Christian teaching and training a direct link between Christian theology and ethics. Or, to put it another way, there is a link between Christian profession and Christian performance. Or, still another way, there is an application of Christian belief called "Christian behavior."

After people have had sound doctrine explained to them, they need to know what suitable behavior is. It is one thing to get the teaching right; it's another thing to get the behavior right. We must teach the truth. We must then help people understand that some kinds of behavior are just not suitable. Some kinds of behavior are, frankly, not in order as far as believers are concerned. And that tremendously powerful link between theology and ethics must be carefully taught.

Now, of course, we are all aware of this, but, unfortunately, it takes us time to understand and accept it. I could give you many illustrations of people who have come to Christ out of a basically pagan background; they really get

There is in all Christian teaching and training a direct link between Christian theology and ethics."

into their Bibles; they understand Christian doctrine; they know the answers to a whole lot of questions. But, strangely, it takes a long time for the old pagan thought patterns to drop away. It takes time for the old pagan entanglements to be disentangled. We often find there's no difficulty at all getting people to study the Epistle to the Philippians, but it's hard getting them to bring behavior patterns into line with the principles they are learning.

That is all part of the Church's responsibility. We are to emphasize that which is suitable to those who understand sound teaching. And we must clearly show people what is improper. There are, after all, things that may be legitimate in a pagan society which, after you purposely and personally identify with Christ, become totally improper. And the new believer needs to make some changes. That is the intent of the training.

To Encourage What Is Strategic

Now, there's another lovely little expression in verse 10 that I want to unearth for you, because it's not sitting on the surface. Talking about how slaves are to behave towards their masters, Paul said to teach them "not to steal from them, but to show that they can be fully trusted, so that in every way they will make the teaching about God our Savior attractive." Notice the emphasis on teaching again.

These slaves have been serving in their Christian community, living in their neighborhood groups, sitting in the Sunday morning service. They're really getting the teaching. The water's available, the oats are salty, and the good old slaves have been coming around and drinking.

But, said the apostle Paul, it is important that they also are trained to behave in such a way that their lives will make the teaching "attractive." Now, isn't that a lovely expression? The word used here is a very fascinating word. It's one that is used to explain what you do with a jewel to show it off to its best advantage.

If you watch the old Westerns, you'll remember the stories of the fellows who got the jewels and put them in a little bag they tied to their belts and stuck in their pockets. That really doesn't show off a jewel to its best advantage. What you have to do with a jewel is give it to somebody who can cut it right, then polish it, and put it in a proper setting. That is the Greek word Paul uses here. He says the responsibility of those who train the Christian fellowship is to get people who understand doctrine to so fit the doctrine into their lives that their lives become the proper setting for the jewel of truth. To me, that is a most delightful concept.

But think of it for a minute. All those people who say, "Don't bother me with doctrine, don't bother me with teaching, don't bother me with theology and all that kind of stuff," really don't understand that we need to be bothered with doctrine and teaching and theology because people need to understand it. Let's face it. Most people aren't going to go to school to learn it. Most people don't want long sermons that teach it. Most people most definitely are satisfied with one dose a week. So they must have it presented to them in a different way. And the apostle Paul says that you present the reality of doctrine and theology in teaching by making sure that your life is a setting for it; that your life is a strategic presentation of it; so that the very life you live becomes a suitable setting for the jewel of truth. Now, that takes a lot of work, a lot of discipline and a lot of help.

It is relatively easy to keep doctrine in the abstract, and theology in an ivory tower. And a lot of us think that the real heavy stuff of the Word of God belongs in the seminaries or to the pastors. However, what the Apostle is telling Titus is, "Go to those Cretans and teach them the truth about God, about man, about salvation, about eternity, about the truth; then get their lives into shape so that their very lives become a setting for the jewel of truth so that it stops being abstract, stops belonging in ivory towers, stops being stuff that seminarians discuss and becomes something very beautiful in the lives of the people." Now that is the intent of training.

Can you see what an enormous task rests upon the Church of Jesus Christ. Can you see the responsibility of the leaders in the Church of Jesus Christ? Their responsibility is to be explaining what is sound, then emphasizing what is suitable, and encouraging people's lives so that they become a strategic setting for the truth of God. And it doesn't happen overnight. It takes a lot of work, a lot of patience, a lot of teaching and a lot of training. Yet, that's what the Church is supposed to be doing.

To Engage What Is Skeptical

Explaining what the older women are supposed to be teaching the younger women, the apostle Paul says in verse 5, that the results will be that, if the younger women do things properly, "No one will malign the Word of God."

There are a lot of people who are skeptical about the Word of God, skeptical about those people who claim to be Christians, or born-again Christians or spirit-filled, born-again Christians—whatever other adjectives we now find necessary. And I think very often they have reason to be skeptical because we make some big claims. We sit in our pews and sing quite happily that we are holy and blameless before the Lord.

Do you believe you're holy? Do you believe you're blameless before God? It is relatively easy for us to use holy clichés and ideas and propagate them without realizing that, when we come out with those clichés and make those statements, there are some people who wander in and who may even be listening. They could say "Those guys really think they are holy and blameless? They've got to be kidding." And they go away and laugh behind our backs and knock and scoff at us and do all kinds of terrible things. And our clichés and professions of faith become the means whereby they begin to rip Christ Himself to shreds.

The apostle Paul said, "Now, we have to get some training here so that we take that opportunity away from them. So that we can know that we are living among skeptical people who are going to level all kinds of criticism at us. As we live among the skeptics, our lives will be so in tune with our doctrine that they will really be hard put to genuinely criticize what we're doing.

Now some people are greatly gifted when it comes to criticism. I sometimes wonder if the gift of criticism isn't the most common gift in the Church of Jesus Christ. I certainly believe that sometimes it is the most ardently exercised gift in the Church. There's no question that everybody can find something to criticize in everybody else sooner or later. But the big thing we've got to realize is that a lot of criticism is grossly unfounded and utterly unfair. And a lot of criticism is more a reflection on the aberrations of the one doing the criticizing than on the person being criticized. Having said all that, our responsibility in training is to do things in such a way that we take away from them the opportunities for skepticism they grasp so seriously.

Then, notice verse 8. Paul tells the young men they have to behave in a certain way, and Titus himself has to model what he is teaching them, "So that those who oppose you may be ashamed because they have nothing bad to say about us." We are to teach people to bring their lives so in tune with their doctrine that the skeptics who live among us will be so frustrated that even though they would love to be able to punch us right in the nose and utterly discredit us, they just can't do it.

There's a newspaper in North Carolina, which, claiming to get at truth, has apparently spent decades looking for ways to discredit Billy Graham. It's very tough for him to take because the newspaper will periodically, regularly, even monotonously, get after him. The interesting thing about it is, though they have tried him at every point and have gone after everything they can, his reputation is still intact. No thanks to the newspaper.

There are plenty of people who will do all they can to besmirch a reputation and rip a character to shreds. The responsibility of those in the Church of Jesus Christ is to know that we live among those kinds of people and we are going to have to take what they give us. But let us teach and train people so that, as God knows our hearts, our detractors are really hard put to find anything that is inconsistent. The responsibility of the Church is to be training people, so that the doctrine they say they have received is being applied in their lives.

The Extent of the Training

Paul gives us some practical clues about the extent of the training.

Managing the People

The Apostle divides the congregation into its rather natu-

ral groupings, which shows that he is actually managing
the people well. He talks about those who are *male* and
those who are *female* because men need one kind of
emphasis and women need another. If you're going to
teach men, you're going to teach them one way. If you're
going to teach women, you're going to have to teach them
another way. Paul obviously recognizes this and he gives
specific instructions on how to train the men and how to
train the women.

He talks about the *young* and the *old*. Young people are
going to go for one thing; old people are going to go for
another. If we're going to train the young people, they're
going to need one kind of emphasis; the old folks probably
won't go for much at all, but we'll try what we can with
them anyway. And he puts a different emphasis there.

Then, of course, there are those who are *deprived, disadvantaged,* and those who were born with a silver spoon
in their mouths. Well, they all have different problems;
they all have different interests; they all have different
prejudices. The have-nots are intent on having what the
haves have, and the haves are intent in insuring that the
have-nots have not what the haves have. That being the
case, Paul says, "We have to recognize that we're going to
have to teach the haves how to handle what they have and
teach the have-nots how to handle what it means to have
not what they have not, and begin to work in these areas."

So, the apostle Paul tells Titus, rightly manage the
people by recognizing the different situations and then
organizing the necessary education for them.

Men, are you letting the Church train you so that your
life is becoming a setting in which the jewel of Christian
doctrine is being beautifully set off, in your factory or your
office? Young people, are you giving the Church the opportunity to so teach and train you that the Christian truth you

learned for many years in your Christian home is ingrained into your life to the extent that your very behavior on the basketball courts, on the football field, in the schoolroom and during recess is such that it is thoroughly consistent with the doctrine?

Women, have you got a handle on teaching, and has the doctrine of God got such a handle on you that people are really very hard put, when they are totally intent on being critical, to find anything to legitimately criticize? Will you give the Church the chance to teach and train you so that the sound truth is getting over to you and the practical application is coming through? That's why the Church is here. We are trying to be God's very own people. It takes a lot of teaching and a lot of training.

Mobilizing the Team

I think when Titus got to Crete and received his instructions from Paul, he probably sent a cable right back and said, "Paul, when you said *all* the towns of Crete, is that what you meant? You mean you want me to do this in all the towns of Crete? How about one of those nice, little towns in Crete?" He said, "There are nice little towns in Crete, Paul. I found myself a nice place here."

"No," Paul said, "I want you to establish churches in all the cities of Crete. I want you to ordain elders in all the cities of Crete."

Titus replied, "I can't do all that. How can I do all that? Only so many hours in the day, you know, Paul."

Paul said, "I know. I didn't tell you to do it yourself. I told you to see that it's done. Get the difference?" Notice the two things Paul immediately tells him.

First, Paul tells him to go and *ordain elders* in every place; elders who themselves are going to teach, train, equip. It was to be a team effort—a team ministry.

One of the greatest disasters in the Church of Jesus Christ in recent years has been this utter fallacy that you pay a pro to do it all. That's why a lot of churches are small. They can't be anything other than small for the very simple reason they have only one person doing it all, and the size of the church is determined by the extent of his energy. When he's out of energy, gas and ideas, the church is out of growth.

On the other hand, when you have a situation where people are managed in different ministries, then a team is being built so that the burden is being shared and the load is being disseminated and authority and opportunity are being delegated, then you are not limited by one man's energy. This has always been the New Testament principle. We lost it for centuries, when somebody dreamed up this clergy and laity dichotomy.

Scriptures are quite clear that those who are elders, those who are pastor-teachers, those who are apostles or prophets, have the responsibility to equip people to do the work of the ministry. Training. Now, the question here is this. Are you in your church appointing elders, equipping leaders? Do you have pastor-teachers who are able to operate in such a way that the immense load of your fellowship is being realistically handled?

But Paul doesn't just talk about the elders. He also talks about *motivating the older women* as well. He says that the older women are to be equipped to have a particular ministry: "Teach the older women to be reverent in the way they live, not to be slanderers or addicted to much wine, but to teach what is good" (v. 3). In other words, it isn't just the male elders who are to have this particular responsibility, but the women have a special responsibility too. And uniquely in this environment and culture, he said

Scriptures are quite clear that those who are elders, those who are pastor-teachers . . . have the responsibility to equip people to do the work of the ministry."

they are to be equipped to train the younger women. The team is taking shape.

"I didn't tell you to do it all yourself, Titus. I didn't tell you to rush around all those cities in Crete and do it all yourself. *Manage* the people properly and then mobilize a team and motivate the people. The evangelical 3M Company!"

Modeling the Truth

People don't just hear what we say. They watch what we do, which is rather an unnerving thought. That's exactly what the apostle Paul says to Titus. "In everything set them an example by doing what is good. In your teaching, show integrity, seriousness and soundness of speech that cannot be condemned" (vv. 7,8). In other words, teach them the truth and model it in your life.

My wife Jill was talking to Ray Stedman's wife one day about this whole business of people's expectations; what people look to you for. She was talking about the sheer pressure of trying to be a role model, knowing her own weaknesses and frailty, her own failures and fallenness, her own sinfulness—the stuff we all cope with. Elaine Stedman said a very helpful thing, and Jill and I have rejoiced in it ever since.

She said, "We're called to be models, Jill. But we're not called to be models of perfection. We're called to be models of growth."

Perfection is what people expect of you and that's tough. Generally, they don't expect it of themselves; they expect it of other people. It's an unrealistic expectation.

But people can rightly expect that those in positions of leadership lead and model the truth in an increasingly mature and valid way. Now, if we are in a position of teaching and training people, we must recognize that what we say will have some impact, but what we do and what we are is probably going to have a much greater impact. If we combine what we are saying with what we are doing and teaching and what we are, then the balance is going to be very powerful indeed. The extent of the teaching requires the modeling of the truth from those who are doing it, *a life-style that is consistent* and *communication that shows real conviction.*

One way you can show conviction in your communication is to give the impression that you know what you're talking about. And if you're trying to teach somebody something, give them the impression that you're prepared, that you've done your homework, that you're not just getting up and shooting from the lip. Far too much of that goes on.

I'm appalled at Saturday night specials. And I'm not talking about handguns. I'm talking about Sunday morning talks that are really Saturday night specials. Last-minute rehashes of the few things teachers know, the few things they've learned. You are going to communicate conviction about that truth if it is perfectly obvious that you have taken the time to figure out what it is and get it across to the people.

Maintaining the Pressure

I'm just going to touch on verse 15 because I will cover it more in the next chapter. Paul says in summary, "These, then, are the things you should teach. Encourage and rebuke with all authority. Do not let anyone despise you."

Notice: In the Church of Jesus Christ, those who are called to oversee, teach, train, equip and lead are required to maintain pressure on the people who are members of the people of God. Maintain pressure on them by a *proper application of the truth.* Sometimes people in the application of the truth need a word of encouragement. Make sure they get it. Other people in the application of the truth need a word of rebuke. Make sure they get it. Other people in the application of the truth need a sense of authority that has been spoken and in those who are presenting truth. Make sure they accept that authority. Paul says, "Don't let anybody schlepp you off, Titus. You're my man there. You're going as a delegate of the apostolic truth."

I've often said to people that Stuart Briscoe, as one of the pastors of Elmbrook Church, has no intrinsic authority. But Stuart Briscoe, when he stands in the pulpit with God's Word, has authority and you'd better believe it. It is not the authority of my person or my position. It is the *authority of God's Word* that I present, and in our teaching and training, we've got to acquire it by maintaining the pressure. And if people need rebuking in the name of the Lord, based on the Word of God, we fail them if we don't rebuke them.

On the other hand, if people need a word of encouragement and we're just pontificating, and there is no personal application, then we're failing them. And if people are simply walking away from a situation and saying, "Get off my back, what's that got to do with you," and we let them get away with it, we're failing them. We are not to let people despise those who minister God's Word. We are not to let people simply shrug their shoulders and disregard those whom God has put in authority over His people; because His people need leadership; and the leadership better know what it's doing. So we'd better *maintain the right pressure.*

The Content of the Training

Paul was aware that different people need to be taught different things depending on their unique circumstances. Accordingly, he instructed Titus to give careful attention to the older men, the older women, the younger women, the younger men, and the slaves whom we will call the disadvantaged. Each group was to be taught the things Paul thought they most needed to hear.

The Older Men

Our society puts a premium on youth and youthfulness. We are familiar with advertising that tries to convince us our gray hair can be turned back imperceptibly to its "natural color" (presumably because gray is unnatural), and pictures showing a couple of lissome beauties in sleek swimsuits sporting identical wide grins full of sparkling teeth, billowing blond hair and sparkling blue eyes, only to be asked to decide which one is the mother of the other! As a result there is a subtle message that "young" is desirable and commendable and "old" is something considerably less. To the extent that Western society has lost sight of the mellow value of older age in the dazzling blaze of youth, our society has lost an asset of experience and maturity that is irreplaceable.

It is true that President Ronald Reagan has reversed the trend to some extent with his considerable youthful vigor but not without the press reminding us that he dozes off in cabinet meetings and papal audiences and needs Nancy's help fielding questions when his hearing aid malfunctions.

Other societies regard older people considerably more highly, a natural progression to the veneration of ancestors. The people Paul was dealing with would, therefore, understand that older men should be respected and this required them to behave with the dignity and maturity that was appropriate to their advancing years. They were to be "temperate, worthy of respect, self-controlled"— meaning that if they expected to be respected they would have to earn respect. This would require discipline on their part. Status and gray hair partially earns respect in some quarters, but inappropriate behavior by older people earns a disproportionate amount of approbation.

My mother had a particular distaste for older people who dressed and behaved younger than their years— "Mutton dressed up as lamb!" she sniffed. Perhaps she had been unduly influenced by her mother who repeatedly told all who would listen, "There's no fool like an old fool!"

The older men were also to ensure that their behavior had a clearly discernible spiritual quality. They were to be sound, that is healthy or robust, in their faith, their love and their endurance. Older people should have a healthy working knowledge of the faith, that is, the theological content of faith, and demonstrate a trusting attitude and a faithful commitment.

Some older people tend to become increasingly self-centered in their later years, but Paul wanted Titus to remind them that they had a lot of love to give and they should seek out those most in need of loving care and support. And, of course, as they grew older and their powers began to wane and their influence began to disappear, the older men could easily become discouraged and defeated. But this must not happen; the older men have much to offer. They must not quit; they must not become self-absorbed; they must not become cranky and disgruntled. They must keep the faith and keep their cool and keep on keeping on.

The Older Women

Turning his attention to the older women, Paul wisely does not define the term "older" but he is most forthright in his instructions, which fall into two categories. First he tells Titus to warn them of weakness and second to channel them to constructiveness. Apparently the older women were spending their time in gossiping, which was slanderous, and over-indulgence in wine tasting. The former would be desperately detrimental to good relationships, the latter patently self-destructive. Gossip has been defined as "sharing something you like about somebody you don't" and, unfortunately, many of us, not just older women, are ill-disciplined in both hearing and speaking the things that are best left unshared. The older women who turned to drink, as many of our modern soap operas document daily, are usually desperately lonely women who have no significant involvement in life. They feel unwanted and useless, grovel in feelings of inferiority and irrelevance, and show their inner disgust and loathing by carefully calculated self-destructive behavior.

These women, in Paul's day, as in ours, need to be channeled into constructive behavior. They need to be taught "reverent" behavior and they, themselves, should become teachers of "what is good." It is worth noting that the word translated "reverent," used only here in the New Testament, means "suitable to a sacred person, service or circumstances" and could possibly refer to an order of older women, *presbutidas*, similar to the "older men"—or elders, *presbuteroi*. Whether or not these women were recognized as leaders in their churches, they were clearly admonished to invest their lives in profitable and honorable behavior.

The Younger Women

The ministry of the older women was to be particularly, but not necessarily exclusively, directed to the younger women. The word "younger" has connotations of "new" or "fresh" and may refer to those women who were "newly" married although not so "freshly" married that they did not have children! The instructions for these women are more numerous than any of the other groups. They are "to love their husbands and children," or literally to be "husband-lovers and children-lovers."

At first sight it might appear unnecessary to train people to do this, as we tend to assume that this kind of love is spontaneous and inevitable. But Paul and Titus, and all other people involved in marriage counseling, know that love in the family is more than a feeling. We all need help in learning how to show love in practical ways and how to love those whose love has grown cold and whose behavior is reprehensible.

How many people have needed help in dealing with wayward and rebellious children? How many broken-hearted young women have not known how to handle their anger and resentment against a drunken, abusive, unfaithful husband? Self-control is something that all age groups need to learn, and Paul mentions it in relation to both older and younger men as well as younger women.

Perhaps the young married woman with small children constantly demanding her attention, and a husband who may be less than sensitive to her special needs, would be prone to irritability and might on occasion give vent to her feelings with a knock-down-drag-out confrontation or an ear-shattering screaming match. Training in how to cope would be most helpful in heading off such potentially catastrophic situations.

"Pure" would certainly include sexual propriety but was much more far-reaching in that it spoke of inner motivation in all areas of life. Young women may be tempted to engage in all kinds of duplicitous and questionable actions because they are limited in what they can do and say. Therefore, when they want to use subterfuge and deceptive manipulation to get their own way they must refrain. "Feminine wiles" and "pure" motivation are hardly compatible.

Most young wives and mothers know that running a household is a major undertaking. Therefore to tell them to be busy at home may seem to be an unnecessary admonition. However, there have always been younger women who have neglected home and children in the same way there have always been older women who drank too much and talked too much. The problem for both would probably be traced to boredom and/or laziness. In some instances younger women have needed home-training because they never learned the practicalities of running a household. In our church we have found that the Young Moms ministry has proven particularly helpful in providing experienced help and encouragement in this specific area.

Of course it is possible to be as busy as a bee and as unsociable as a hornet. Martha of Bethany, for example, who while she was busy doing what she felt necessary, was becoming quite resentful about her busyness and irritated with all who got in her path. The answer to that is to teach a kind spirit. Perhaps this can be done best by elevating the value of running a home and family in the popular perception and being careful to express appreciation for all that the hard-working homemaker does. Perhaps husbands and children could encourage the young mothers to kindness by being helpful and appreciative themselves, at least occasionally!

The final instruction relates to husband-wife relations with particular reference to the wives being "subject to their husbands." While this instruction is the cause of much debate in our modern society it would cause no debate in Paul's day for the simple reason that in first-century society women were given no other option than to be subject to their husbands, since they were regarded as little more than property and chattels. We need, therefore, to ask why Paul would make such a point of female submission and, in other places, male headship, seeing it was a foregone conclusion. The answer would appear to be that the unique emancipation that the Christian gospel had brought to women may well have led to an attitude among the women that was less than respectful to their menfolk and, accordingly, scandalous to the secular society. If Paul's instruction was mildly surprising to the women, his instruction that men should love their wives as Christ loved the Church was revolutionary, and his teaching on men and women subjecting themselves to each other was positively mind-boggling! (See Eph. 5:21-25.)

Paul and Titus were well aware of the radical societal changes the gospel was introducing, and they recognized that too many changes too soon could cause a backlash effect, which, in turn, would give their opponents an opportunity to "malign the word of God." Rather than allow that to happen, God's people have always found it necessary to govern their behavior and even, at times, curtail their own legitimate freedoms for the sake of the gospel.

The Younger Men

Surprisingly the younger men were to be taught only one thing and that was to be "self-controlled." As we have seen, the same instruction was to be given to other people as well, but perhaps it was necessary to mention only self-control because if young men got a handle on that the rest would be relatively easy for them. Being men, of course, they had far more freedom than the women, who were secluded in their homes, discouraged from appearing in public, not allowed to work outside the home and generally treated in a manner similar to that practiced by fundamentalist Muslims in their homes. The more freedom granted, the more self-control is needed.

Being young also necessitates self-control and the two are not easy bedfellows! "Youthful exuberance," "high spirits," "fun-loving" are all common terms, some euphemistic, which not infrequently describe irresponsible, destructive and abusive behavior. Granted, much of it is unthinking and benign, but careful training helps even young people look before they leap, thus saving them from the malignant effects of benign youthful intentions.

The Slaves—or the Disadvantaged

If the gospel brought new status and opportunity to first-century women, young and old alike, it also introduced the seeds from which the full flower of the emancipation of slaves flourished. The Hebrews had always adhered to strict rules concerning the ownership and treatment of slaves, many aspects of which served not only to alleviate their suffering but also, in many instances, to rescue the unfortunate from penury and even starvation. The same could not always be said for the slaves of other cultures, and the gospel message with its emphasis on God's concern for the humble and the poor and their exalted position in the eternal kingdom came to them like a breath of sweet, fresh air after the dank odors of a fetid prison cell.

But in the same way the younger women needed to be trained not to abuse new freedoms, the slaves needed to be taught how to behave as spiritually emancipated, yet socially disenfranchised, people. Their instructions all dealt with their relationships to their masters. They were to be "subject" to them, which, of course, was not new as the women's mandatory subjection to their men. The slaves were placed in a position of enforced subjection and servitude. The difference, however, was that they would subject themselves voluntarily from the heart as opposed to the surly, uncooperative kind of subjection that is so common among those who are powerless. This would be shown in the genuine desire "to try to please" their masters.

Note that they are "to try to please," which is a very realistic instruction given the fact it is impossible to please some people. Evidently, slaves had become so truculent because of their underprivileged status that it was common for them to "talk back" to the masters and, whenever they had the chance, to "steal from them." It would, no doubt, be easy for them to rationalize such behavior both on the grounds it was common practice and because it was the only way they could compensate for the abuse they were suffering.

Christian slaves, however, had a higher and nobler concern—they were to "make the teaching about God our Savior attractive." One way they would do this was by showing that they could be "fully trusted."

In many ways slavery has long since vanished from the scene and the advent of the Christian gospel had much to do with its demise, but racial discrimination is still with us, abuse of the underprivileged is not uncommon, the powerless are still dominated. And the gospel still applies in two ways. Those who serve a God of justice need to represent

Him to and on behalf of the disadvantaged, and the Christians among the disadvantaged need to be encouraged to live well in their circumstances until such time as the slow moving wheels of change make life more pleasant and just for everyone. In so doing they cannot help but make the gospel attractive, because nothing calls attention to the message of grace quicker than gracious living under pressure.

Questions for further study _____

1. What is the monumental task given to Titus by the apostle Paul? How is that task still important in our churches today?
2. What are the specific groups of people spoken about in the second chapter of Titus? And what is the distinct emphasis in training that relates to each group?
3. One of the key factors, according to the author, in the intent of training of God's people is emphasizing what is suitable, or what is becoming. In other words, what Christians profess should match up with their performance as believers. How does what you profess match up to your Christian conduct?
4. According to the apostle Paul, what has more impact, what we say, or what we do? Does your life-style model what your lips speak?

CHAPTER FIVE

Purifying God's People

I. God's people problem

A. Active in ungodliness

B. Attracted to worldly passions

C. Anchored in the present age

D. Antagonistic in wickedness

II. God's perfect project

A. The epiphany events like towers

1. The epiphany of grace
2. The epiphany of glory

B. The salvation experiences like cables

1. The experience of redemption
2. The experience of sanctification

III. God's purifying procedure

A. The educational process

1. Edification by grace
2. Application by man

B. The expectation factor

C. The enthusiasm factor

Titus 2:11-15

For the grace of God that brings salvation has appeared to all men. It teaches us to say "No" to ungodliness and worldly passions, and to live self-controlled, upright and godly lives in this present age, while we wait for the blessed hope—the glorious appearing of our great God and Savior, Jesus Christ, who gave himself for us to redeem us from all wickedness and to purify for himself a people that are his very own, eager to do what is good. These, then, are the things you should teach. Encourage and rebuke with all authority. Do not let anyone despise you.

I probably spent more time studying these few verses of Scripture than any other I've studied for quite some time, because the more I got into this passage, the more thrilled I became with the tremendous weight of truth there is to be found here. I will touch on some of the more salient points, but I hope that what I'm able to share will only stimulate your desire to get into this passage for yourself, because it is so rich in spiritual truth.

If you go to the Golden Gate in San Francisco, you will see a narrow inlet; it's two miles across and four miles long. On each side of the inlet, there are rather steep hills, and a deep channel comes through the strait. The strait opens up on one side, of course, to the Pacific Ocean and on the other side to San Francisco Bay. Because a lot of traffic wanted to get from the San Francisco peninsula to Northern California, and vice versa, they used to have to travel all the way around the bay. So somebody came up with a great idea. They decided they would try to bridge the gap. They built something we are all familiar with, something all the tourists want to see no matter where they come from: the famous Golden Gate Bridge.

Now, those of you who are familiar with the outline of the Golden Gate Bridge know that it is supported on only two towers. Fastened to these towers are massive cables, and from these massive cables are all kinds of other cables on which the bridge is suspended. That, strangely enough, is why they call it a suspension bridge. The problem with a suspension bridge, of course, even though it is a marvelous way to bridge a great distance like the Golden Gate, if the wind blows, the cables can begin to swing; sometimes these bridges collapse in high winds.

Those who have been in the army also know that if you are marching in a platoon and come to a suspension bridge, you are given the order to break step, because if you march in step across a suspension bridge, the momentum and the rhythm could bring the thing crashing down. Now, I want you to know about the Golden Gate Bridge because this may be an illustration that will help you understand what it is Paul is telling Titus to teach the people of Crete.

You see, God has a lot of people standing on one side of a deep chasm and He wants to get them on to the other side. But He has a problem: how to bridge the gap. Now, if we can rightly understand the ministry of Christ and the Christian Church, we have to understand where people are, where God wants to take them and the bridge He is going to use to get them there. That's what Paul talks about here.

God's People Problem

Let's get hold of this idea of God's people problem—the real situation as we confront it, or more importantly, as God confronts it today. Notice four things this passage of Scripture tells us about the situation mankind is in. In verse 12 we are told of ungodliness, worldly passions, and a mention of this present age. Those are three terms that bear careful looking into. Then, in verse 14, there is another key word, "wickedness." Those four terms—ungodliness, worldly passions, present age and wickedness—clearly describe the situation of humanity as God sees it on one side of the chasm that separates us from our Lord.

Active in Ungodliness

Ungodliness means that we have an attitude of heart and an activity in life-style that clearly demonstrate we are not serious about God. The Greek word used here is the exact opposite from the word *godly* that occurs so often in the pastoral Epistles. God wants people to be godly. The root idea of that word is "to take God seriously." The problem, God says, with our society and with our lives, is that we do not take Him seriously and we exhibit this in the activities we find so attractive.

Attracted to Worldly Passions

Worldly passions is tied in with the expression *the present age,* and are really two biblical terms for what we call today in modern parlance *secularism.* The word *secular* is related to the idea of world, and it has to do with an attitude of heart, mind and life-style that show we are more interested in the age in which we live than in the age to come. And we are fundamentally more attracted to a life that is rooted in the material things in this world than we are concerned about the spiritual things of the world to come.

Anchored in the Present Age

Webster's Dictionary has a marvelous definition of secularism: Secularism is a system of social ethics based upon a doctrine that ethical standards and conduct should be determined exclusively with reference to the present life and social well-being, without reference to religion.

In other words, there is a system of social ethics in our world based on the idea that all that really matters is social well-being now, and the age in which we're living, without any reference to eternity, God, or as Webster's puts it, without any reference to religion at all.

Antagonistic in Wickedness

Secularism is an attitude of the mind that produces an ethic for individuals and society as a whole that carefully and calculatedly rules out God, eternity, absolute standards, and has nothing whatsoever to do with Christian ethics.

That is the situation in which we find our society today. There's nothing new about it; it has always been the case. Now, different societies at different times have been able to disguise this rather carefully and cleverly. But the interesting thing that's happening at the present time is that we are no longer bothering to disguise it. It is abundantly clear that the basic approach to life in the society of which we are part is that they have an ethic that is determined exclusively with reference to the present life, the social well-being, without any reference whatsoever to God, eternity or absolute values. And there is evidence of this on every hand.

I had a free evening not so long ago, which in itself was something of an experience for me. The telephone didn't ring; no one came by. I was so taken aback by this unusual situation that I sat down, switched on the television and spent one of the most depressing, boring evenings of my life. I went to bed with a heavy burden on my heart for all the dear people in this country who have nothing better to do than to watch television.

Now, I'm not going to start a rampage against television. I like the news; I like the sports; and I like, quite frankly, PBS, because they show a lot of BBC programs— if you'll pardon that expression. But the utter emptiness, the utter deadness of what was being presented, coupled with what's even more important, a philosophy and an ethic that has absolutely no interest whatsoever in God, eternity or absolute values, was unbelievably depressing.

I was discussing my dismay with somebody who asked, "Have you watched the afternoon soaps lately?"

I said, "I haven't watched an afternoon soap in years."

She said, "Watch a few sometime. If anything, they're even worse."

What is our television doing? It is simply portraying our society. And we know perfectly well that because society operates on the profit motive, it is giving us exactly what we want. What does that say about our society? Nothing more than we have become tremendously active in our ungodliness, that we are deeply attracted to secularism, that we are anchored in this present age. And the result is that we are simply spewing out utter wickedness, and an unwillingness to go with God's principles and do things His way.

This is only one illustration of the situation facing us. We've got a problem. And God has a problem, because He is God, sitting on one side of a deep chasm that separates man from Himself. We are a society that is characterized by ungodliness, rooted in this present age, governed by worldly passions, spewing out wickedness.

Now, God wants to address this society and bring out of it a people for Himself. What a lovely expression that is. That in essence is the genius of the Church: It is God moving into that situation and bringing out of it a very special people who are clearly, demonstrably His very own people. The struggle we confront is that it is very difficult to get a lot of people out of that situation. But probably more important to us right now is the fact that a lot of people are still very much governed by the very attitudes, attractions and activities they profess to have left.

The ministry of the Christian Church is not only to get to people where they are and bring them across the bridge God has built into His people, but it is also to keep people moving in the process of getting out from where they were into what God wants them to be—God's very own people. And what a burden this is. What a tremendous responsibility for the Church. Because we are so swamped with ungodliness and attitudes that are utterly wicked, because they are rooted in worldly passions in this present age, very often we don't even know how much we are governed by them. We don't even know how much our thinking and our ethics and our activities are simply modeling that which is contrary to all that God is. That's God's people problem.

God's Perfect Project

What is God going to do about this situation? Getting back

to our illustration of the Golden Gate Bridge, we can answer this question. Remember those two towers? As you read this passage of Scripture in Titus, you'll see standing out of it two great big towers. And they are identified by the word "appeared" or "appearing." The word, strictly in theology, is *epiphany,* an anglicization of the Greek word used here. I want you to note this word very carefully. In verse 11, Paul says, "The grace of God that brings salvation has appeared." Then you'll notice in verse 13 he says, "While we wait for the blessed hope—the glorious appearing."

The Epiphany Events Standing Like Towers

I want to suggest that God, intent on reaching His problem people, is building a bridge to get them from where they are to where He wants them to be. And He's doing it by building two great towers called, for want of a better term, our "epiphany towers." Now, let me explain the meaning behind epiphany, or appearance. In one sense it can be used to describe the sudden burst of light that happens at sunrise. I've often taken overnight flights around the world. And one of the greatest moments is when, instead of the imperceptible dawn coming, the sun suddenly bursts over the horizon. Now, that is strictly an epiphany in the sense in which the Greeks used it. It means a sudden appearance.

But the idea was taken and used in many different ways. For instance, the Caesars of those days would use epiphany to describe a majestic, dramatic appearance of themselves in a certain situation. When Queen Elizabeth II toured the U.S. West Coast, it was interesting to see the response on the part of many people. They recognized something of majesty, awe, something indefinable about her. And when she appeared, the people gathered around and, with some exceptions of course, seemed to be pleased to see her. Now then, this was an appearance, an epiphany, a majestic, dramatic appearance.

God has planned two majestic, dramatic appearances and they are the towers of the bridge He is building. The first one is an historical epiphany; it has already happened. The second one is an eschatological appearance; it is yet to happen.

The first tower is the *epiphany of grace*. The grace of God that brings salvation has appeared to all men. The thrust here is that God, in grace, has majestically and dramatically intervened in the affairs of man.

Now grace is a term with which we are familiar. We hear it quite often. Let me remind you that it really means "God's unmerited favor which comes from His unsolicited choice." Mankind, ungodly, wrapped up in worldly passions, rooted in the present age, enjoying her wickedness, making excuses for it, is not particularly interested in getting to God and saying, "God, please intervene." God's intervention in the human condition far predates man's desire for anything different. The reason God intervened in the human condition is quite simply because, unsolicited and unmerited, He determined to give us what we didn't deserve. It was His free choice; it was His initiative; He decided to do it.

The epiphany of grace, this unmerited favor of God, was dramatically and majestically portrayed in the Incarnation. Our Lord Jesus laid aside His glory, assumed our humanity, and dramatically appeared on earth. For 30 years He was dramatically present among us. For three years He was majestically, dramatically among us, demonstrating God in the flesh. At the end of those 33 years, He dramatically and majestically laid down His life. On the

third day, He dramatically and majestically rose again from
the dead, showed Himself openly, and in so doing, showed
what God was prepared to give us, for no other reason
than He chose to be gracious to us.

Incarnation, crucifixion, resurrection—these are the
terms that come under the heading of the great tower of
the epiphany of grace. What God has chosen to do about
the human condition is built on that first tower. He has
chosen to give us the Incarnation. He has chosen to give
us the Crucifixion. He has chosen to give us the Resurrection. It is a ministry of grace. But it is not only a ministry
of grace, it is a ministry that demonstrates the greatness
of God, which is utterly unlimited.

Verse 13 talks about "the glorious appearing of our
great God and Savior." But not only that, it speaks of the
gift of God that is utterly uninhibited. For it tells us that in
the epiphany of grace this great God and Savior "gave himself for us" (Titus 2:14). So what is the tower on which
God is building this bridge to get people from where they
are to where He wants them to be? It is the tower of
grace. The grace of God has dramatically, majestically
appeared, culminating in the great God and Savior, our
Lord Jesus giving Himself to redeem us. That is fundamental to Christian truth. That is the tower on which the
whole bridge is suspended.

But you can't suspend a bridge on one tower. There
have to be two. Accordingly, there are two epiphanies.
The one historical, the epiphany of grace. The second
tower is eschatological, the *epiphany of glory*. And Paul
tells Titus that those who understand the grace of God and
are thrilled by it and say, "God, how wonderful that you
should deal with us in grace," are characterized by a certain looking forward to the other epiphany. They are people who because of their excitement in what God has done

in grace, are excited about what God is going to do to finalize all He has in mind.

What is He going to do? He has planned another dramatic, majestic epiphany, an appearance. In the same way that the sun bursts on the dawn and gives light to the world, so our Lord Jesus having once burst into our world, majestically and dramatically, will do it again. This event is called by many the Second Coming. And in Scripture we are clearly taught that our Lord Jesus who has come will also come again. That is the second tower.

God has promised that a great and glorious day will come in which our risen Lord Jesus will appear. He will appear in great glory. He will come with all the majesty of heaven clearly upon His brow, attended by the angels of glory. And it will be a great and glorious and terrible day of the Lord.

Joel 2:31 says, "The sun will be turned to darkness and the moon to blood before the coming of the great and dreadful day of the LORD." This is a prophetic statement by the prophet concerning the great appearing of our Lord Jesus Christ. In Acts 2 you will find that the very expressions used in Joel are quoted by Peter on the day of Pentecost. But, there's a subtle difference. Acts 2:19-20 says, "I will show wonders in the heaven above and signs on the earth below, blood and fire and billows of smoke. The sun will be turned to darkness and the moon to blood before the coming of the great and glorious day of the Lord."

Do you notice the difference? In Joel His appearance is called the great and dreadful day of the Lord; in Acts, the great and glorious day of the Lord. It doesn't mean they are two different events. It just means that, like most things, there are two different ways of looking at it.

When Jesus Christ comes again in the glorious epiphany, in that dramatic, majestic appearance, when like the

God has promised that a great and glorious day will come in which our risen Lord Jesus will appear."

sun He bursts on the scene once again, for some people it will be the most glorious thing that ever happened. For others it will be the most dreadful thing they could ever imagine. Why? Because the day of the Lord will spell glory and blessing for some and untold judgment for others. If you have discovered the meaning of grace and the wonder of what God has given you in Christ, then you have *responded* to His grace and have decided to step off the peninsula and onto the bridge. And as you walk onto the bridge, you will come to that first tower of the epiphany of grace, and you will say, "God, in your great glory and majesty, you have dramatically given us Christ. I put my trust in Him." And then you keep on walking across the bridge looking for the second tower when the One you have trusted will come again to take you to be with Himself for all eternity. This is what Paul in Titus 2:13 calls, "The blessed hope."

Now, when the Bible talks about the blessed hope, it doesn't mean wishful thinking. It means the sheer confidence that comes when you know the One whom you have believed. You have stepped off the peninsula, where you have a life characterized by ungodliness and worldly passions anchored in the present day, spewing out wickedness. You have committed yourself to Christ and are starting across the bridge, approaching rapidly that second tower when the great and dreadful day of the Lord will come. That day, if you are trusting Christ, will be glory all the way. If you are rejecting Christ, it will be a great and dreadful day of the Lord.

For when He comes in great glory, every knee will bow to Him and every tongue will confess Him as Lord (see Isa. 45:23; Rom. 14:11; Phil. 2:10). Those who do it willingly are those who understand the message of grace. Those who reject the message of grace will be forced to do it, but they will never be forced into heaven. The second coming of our Lord Jesus, which we keenly anticipate, is the second tower on which the bridge has been built.

So, God's project to deal with His problem people is, first of all, to build two towers: the epiphany of grace and the epiphany of glory, the historical appearance and the eschatological appearance. They are solidly build. One happened; one assuredly will happen. This is the basis of our faith.

The Salvation Experiences Suspended Like Cables

Suspended on these two towers are two cables on which everything hangs. Titus 2:14 says that our Lord Jesus, the great God and Savior, "Gave himself for us to redeem us from all wickedness." That's the first cable. It is the experience of redemption. It goes on to say that He gave Himself also "To purify for himself a people that are his very own." This is the cable of sanctification.

So, you have two towers—the first epiphany and the second epiphany and strung on those two towers are the two cables—the cable of redemption and the cable of sanctification.

First, the *cable of redemption*. What does redemption mean? Notice the expression used here, He "gave himself for us to redeem us" is very similar to an expression found in 1 Timothy 2:6: "[He] gave himself as a ransom for all men—the testimony given in its proper time." The idea of redemption, ransom, runs strongly through New Testament teaching. What does it mean? I think we're all familiar with what sometimes happens when somebody is kidnapped, the kidnappers demand a ransom. Our Lord Jesus Christ was dealing with a whole lot of kidnapped people. If we can mix the metaphor, these kidnapped people are on that peninsula. They're stuck out there in their ungodliness and their wickedness. They're really drowned by their worldly passions in their present age, and somehow or another, they have to be brought out of the situation they are in.

The big question is, What is the ransom price? And the Scriptures tell us that the price is our Lord Jesus Christ giving Himself as a ransom. If you check Titus 2:14, there are two little words that are very important indeed. One tells us that our Lord gave Himself on *behalf* of us. The other little word tells us that our Lord gave Himself *instead* of us. So when we talk in terms of the cost of our redemption, we are reminded of the cross; our Lord Jesus Christ willingly giving Himself instead of us, on our behalf that we might be liberated from that which binds us, that we may enjoy release.

The second aspect of redemption found here is a word that was used in the slave markets in New Testament days. When a slave would be standing on the block, someone would come along and pay the price for him. The purchaser would then take the chains off the slave's hands and feet, take him by the hand and lead him away into a new experience. So, our Lord Jesus, giving Himself instead of us, giving Himself on behalf of us, does it in order that He might release us from our present situations and lead us onto the bridge. And as He leads us onto the bridge, He has one thing in mind: He wants us to become part of His very own people. That's one of the cables, the cable of redemption.

The other is the *cable of sanctification.* For He is not just interested in paying a ransom in order that He might release us, He is interested in doing something even more than that. He wants to bring us into an experience of sanctification. Now, the word used here is to "purify." Purifying for Himself a people that are His very own.

If you look into the expression, "A people that are His very own," you find another rich word. It means a very special possession. And it's an expression taken from the Old Testament. You can pick it up in Exodus 19:5 where Jehovah says that the people of Israel are a very special people, uniquely His own. The idea runs right through the Old Testament; but it's taken up in the New Testament, not of the people of Israel now, but of the Church of Jesus Christ.

So, when we think of sanctification we have to realize this first of all: When our Lord Jesus works redemption in our lives, He also works in sanctification. For, if He leads us out of the slave market by paying the ransom, we become His own. Or as the apostle Paul puts it in 1 Corinthians 6:19,20, "You are not your own; you were bought at a price."

Now, that's something God's people have to get hold of. Because, you see, sometimes in our society we invite people to pray to receive Christ. That's a simple little expression. Or we ask people to invite Jesus into their hearts. That's another simple expression. It's relatively easy to get people to pray that prayer or to say they'll ask Jesus into their hearts. But that's inadequate. What we've got to explain to people is this. "Listen, if you experience redemption, you're automatically involved in sanctification. For, if Christ in redemption pays the ransom for you, then He in sanctification possesses you as His own. You have clearly become His."

Now, the reason I stress this is that you can get people to pray to receive Christ without their having any thought of becoming Christ's; they like to be their own. It's relatively easy to get people to pray a prayer that is going to help them out of a situation without facing the fact that now they belong to Jesus. And Jesus belongs to them. You can't build a bridge on one tower. And you can't swing a bridge on one cable. There is the cable of redemption where we are ransomed, but there is also the cable of sanctification where we are possessed.

So, this is how we make people of God: We tell them about the epiphanies—the towers—and teach them about the cables—the experiences of redemption and sanctification.

But, let's go back to the picture of the slave. The ransom has been paid; the slave is taken to live in the master's house. What has to be done first? You have to clean him up. There has to be a purifying process. Now, this is all part of the work of the Church of Jesus Christ. For sanctification means, on one hand, that we have been set apart for God and we are owned by Him; but sanctification on the other hand means, now we're owned by Him and we must clean up our act.

Notice, we don't have to get our act cleaned up to come to Him. But, when we come to Him it's on the understanding that our act is going to get cleaned up. This has to be stressed in our society. It's not too difficult to get people whose act is in a mess to come to Jesus, and then, having come to Him, continue on in their old act. That's not it. We've got to get the people whose act is in a mess and tell them about redemption—that Jesus, in grace, gave His very self on their behalf that He might purchase them to Himself; and having done that, they should then be prepared to have Him also clean up their act. That is sanctification.

So what is God's perfect project? His project is to bridge the gap between where people are and where He wants them to be. How does He do it? First, He builds the tower of the appearance of grace—it has happened. Then

He builds a second tower, the appearance of glory—it will happen. Then on those two towers He strings the cable of redemption where it is possible for people to be ransomed from their sin and released from their situation; then He strings the cable of sanctification where, having been released from their situation, they become His very own, and He begins to clean up their act. This is the bridge that is being built.

God's Purifying Procedure

We now have people who understand the process and they've started on the way, well off the old peninsula, and are going through the process, but what do we do with them?

The Educational Process

First, the educational process has to be built into people. Paul says the grace of God "teaches us to say 'No'" (Titus 2:12). In other words, when I understand the grace of God, I am exposing myself to the *edification process of grace.*

I believe that one of the great needs among believers is to understand the grace of God. This idea of God's unmerited favor, His uninhibited giving and unlimited power made available to us for no other reason than that He chose to do it, is something that ought to grip our hearts. It ought to edify our hearts. Why? Well, if I understand that grace led Christ to give Himself in my stead, and if I understand that grace led Christ to give Himself on behalf of me, that it was necessary for Him to do all this because of my ungodliness and my wickedness and my worldly passions and my being anchored in the present

The grace of God teaches us to say no to ungodliness and worldly passions, but also to say yes to living self-controlled, upright and godly lives."

age, if I understand that, I say, "God, I just can't go back to these worldly passions. God, if grace has brought me out of all that, I can't go back into that." If the grace of God has moved into my life and dragged me out of that peninsula, why should I drag myself back into it? The grace of God has appeared and because it has burst into my life dramatically, majestically, like the sunrise, it teaches me that I just can't go back to the old life. It teaches me to say no.

This is the beginning of the purification process. This is where some of us need to begin. Some of us need to start taking this more seriously. It is the ultimate insult to say that grace redeemed me, took me from where I was, but I don't want to stay here so I spend all my time heading back.

The edification process of grace teaches us when to say no to ungodliness and to worldly passions. If we have become utterly riddled with secular thinking and an attitude that doesn't take God seriously, we have to acknowledge these attitudes are wrong, and every time they appear—because of grace—we'll say no to them. That's the purification process.

Not only that, we've got to learn how to say yes as well. For the grace of God teaches us to say no to ungodliness and worldly passions, but also to say yes to living self-controlled, upright and godly lives. These three words are very common in the pastoral Epistles and they point to the way we should look at ourselves, our self-controlled attitude towards God and towards people. We've got to say yes to a different attitude toward ourselves, yes to a different attitude toward God, yes to a different attitude toward people.

This is the edification process and it is the responsibility of the Church of Jesus Christ to see that people have entered into it. Grace edifies. God's men and women *apply the edification.* That's why Paul says in verse 15 that Titus should teach these things. Encourage people to say no. Rebuke people when they don't say no. And do it with authority. What authority? The authority that comes because you are built on the towers, suspended on the cables and are on the bridge that God has built. Rebuke people for not saying yes when they should. Encourage people to say yes when they must, and do it all with authority. This is all part of the purification process.

The Expectation Factor

The Bible says that those who believe that Christ will come again believe in a glorious appearing. And there are those who, according to 2 Timothy 4:8, long for His appearing. I have heard of some really getting excited about Jesus coming again. Sometimes that's because their life down here is so hard they want to get out. I understand that. I don't think that's what Paul is talking about though. What he's talking about is that we're so excited about the appearing of grace—what happened when Christ first appeared—that we long for His coming and bringing to consummation all that He started, really finishing off all that He began. And the thing that really excites us is that the last time He came it was a crucifixion, but the next time He comes it will be a coronation.

The Enthusiasm Factor

The expectation of that dramatic, glorious appearing will govern the way we behave. It has a great purifying effect upon us. But then there's the enthusiasm factor too. For when we understand the bridge and what God has done, when we see what He's done in our lives, then we antici-

Purifying God's People 141

pate with enthusiasm the great and glorious and dreadful day of the Lord. And you know how we show it? We are a people who are eager to do what is good!

If I were to come to you sometime and say, "Tell me, what is your ambition?" I wonder what you'd say. I often ask people, "What would you really like to be?" Do you know what the most beautiful answer could be? "I'd like to be good. I'd really like to be good."

Questions for further study _____

1. What, according to our author, is God's people problem? What four terms identify the situation of humanity as God sees it?
2. The epiphany of *grace* and the epiphany of *glory* are the two towers God has erected upon which to bridge the gap between fallen mankind and Himself. Explain what each of the epiphanies means to you.
3. The cables on which our salvation experience suspends are the cables of *redemption* and *sanctification*. Explain what the cables mean to you.
4. What factors make up the purifying procedure of God's people? As you list the factors, think about how each of these applies to your own life.

CHAPTER SIX

Reminding God's People

I. How they used to live

A. In relation to God

1. Darkened in understanding
2. Disobedient to revealed truth

B. In relation to self

1. Deceived by misinformation
2. Dominated by self-centeredness

C. In relation to others

1. Distorted by reactions
2. Discouraged by opposition
3. Destroyed by attitudes

II. How they were saved

A. Not all people are God's people

B. All God's people are saved people

1. Salvation is an act
2. Salvation is a fact
3. Salvation is a pact

III. How they behave

A. In terms of authority

B. In terms of charity

C. In terms of integrity

D. In terms of dignity

Titus 3:1-5

Remind the people to be subject to rulers and authorities, to be obedient, to be ready to do whatever is good, to slander no one, to be peaceable and considerate, and to show true humility toward all men. At one time we too were foolish, disobedient, deceived and enslaved by all kinds of passions and pleasures. We lived in malice and envy, being hated and hating one another. But when the kindness and love of God our Savior appeared, he saved us, not because of righteous things we had done, but because of his mercy.

These verses start off with the word *remind*. In the original language, that word is in the present tense; therefore, it means literally, "go on reminding." And memory is a phenomenal part of our humanity.

I once read a case history of a man who, because of an error during brain surgery, had the wrong part of his brain removed so that his memory was totally destroyed. He was able to function in all other areas, but without memory. That meant that every time he picked up a newspaper he read it as if he'd never seen one before. And every time he met a person, he met that person as if he'd never seen him before. Every time he heard a piece of music he heard it as if hearing it for the first time. Every action he engaged in was as if it had never happened before. Every moment of his life was spent in relearning. That was quite an arresting thought to me, because I realized how much we depend on memory.

If we didn't have memory, we would spend every moment of our lives relearning. But because we do have memory, we can store up the things we have learned; we can accumulate experience. Then we can recall the experience and knowledge we have, and build upon them at any given moment, so that our lives are filled not with relearning but with responding to the accumulation of experience.

Memory, accordingly, enriches our lives unbelievably. However, we do have a problem with memory because if your memory is like mine, it is the thing we forget with! And I'm afraid I do tend to forget things. Now, we forget things for a number of reasons. One of the reasons is that there is a slow erosion going on inside the brain called "aging." You may have heard the story of the professor who got up to lecture his students: "I'm going to speak to you today on the subject of senility. There are three causes of senility. The first is forgetfulness and I've forgotten the other two."

Your memory can begin to go because you're getting older and some of the brain power you have isn't quite what it used to be. Your memory can also go because you just don't want to remember; and there's no question but that we are often capable of putting out of our minds the things we don't want to remember. That is why it is so important we have memory aids built into our lives.

It is interesting to notice how often Scripture insists that, as far as spiritual experience is concerned, we need to go on being reminded. Now, you remember that the Lord Jesus, when He was speaking to His disciples shortly before His departure, told them that the Holy Spirit would come. And that the ministry of the Holy Spirit, among many other things, would be to bring things to their remembrance (see John 14:26).

Not only that, Scripture often speaks to those in positions of Christian leadership and Christian responsibility and tells them that a major part of their responsibility is to go on reminding people. Why? Because if we are to mature spiritually, we don't do it by relearning every time we are in a spiritual situation; we mature spiritually by being able to recall that which we have accumulated in terms of truth and experience over the years. We build on it and we mature because of our response to it.

But, sometimes we just don't bother to remember. Sometimes we let other pieces of information crowd out the things we know. And sometimes we try hard to repress the knowledge we have in our spiritual experience. Accordingly, the Apostle tells Titus it is imperative that he go on reminding the people of certain things.

England's Dr. Samuel Johnson once said, "It is not adequately understood that men more often need to be reminded than instructed." And, quite frankly, when we look at our own spiritual experience, I think many of us would have to admit that we don't need new experiences, more information and new truths. What we need is constant reminders to bring experience into line with the truth we have already been given.

Reminding God's People How They Used to Live

There are three things in this passage of Scripture I want to draw to your attention concerning what we need to be reminded of. For instance, it's interesting to notice that the apostle Paul includes himself and Titus and the Cretans in pointing out how God's people used to live. Notice in verse 3, he says "At one time we too." By using the expression "we too" he is including himself and Titus along with the inhabitants of Crete, before they had a living experience of the living God.

It is important, said the apostle Paul, to go on reminding people who claim to be disciples of Christ what they used to be like. There is a sense in which we don't want to go on harking back to what we used to be like; we need to be putting these things behind us. In fact, the apostle Paul in Philippians 3:13 does say, "Forgetting what is behind and straining toward what is ahead." He is not suggesting to Titus that Christians ought to be constantly raking through the ashes of former experiences; but he is saying that it is healthy for us, if we are to be maturing spiritually, to have some sense of orientation. And that orientation comes through knowing where we used to be. Why? Because if we are maturing spiritually there ought to be some considerable distance between where we are now and where we used to be. We will only be able to measure that distance if we know how to look at where we used to be.

So we need to remind ourselves of where we used to live before we had an experience of the living God in His Son, our Lord Jesus. There are three areas as far as this is concerned: (1) in relation to God; (2) in relation to ourselves; and (3) in relation to others.

In Relation to God

"At one time we too were foolish" (v. 3). That is an expression that talks about our relationship to God. In contemporary idiom, when we talk about people being fools or being foolish, we mean something different from

If we are maturing
spiritually there ought to be
some considerable distance
between where we are now
and where we used to be."

what they meant in New Testament times. Then it meant a person who was devoid of knowledge, of sensitivity as far as God was concerned. You remember the famous expression in the Old Testament that says "The fear of the LORD is the beginning of knowledge" (Prov. 1:7). In other words, the knowledge of the Lord is the fundamental basis of all real knowledge.

Conversely, if we do not fear, know or acknowledge the Lord, then we are lacking in that which gives us real knowledge and real wisdom. Not knowing Him, or honoring Him, or recognizing the Lord is, in essence, what the Bible means by foolishness. It means that I may have all kinds of information stored up in my head, all kinds of diplomas hung on my wall and all kinds of accolades from my society, but if at the root of my being I do not know God as God, or recognize His truth as being truth, all the data, all the diplomas and all the acclaim are, in the end, of relatively small value. For what makes everything else make sense is that God is the originator of all things; that He is the One who is the consummation of all things. If I take God out of these things, all the data doesn't make sense at all.

Now, the apostle Paul says to Titus, You and I and all these people in Crete at one time were darkened in our understanding about life. And the reason was that we didn't know God. Because we didn't know God, we didn't understand that all things are created. Because we didn't know God, we didn't know that all things are upheld by His mighty power. Because we didn't know God, we had no sense of purpose. Because we didn't know God, we had no idea of the eternal significance of life. Because we didn't know God, we did not understand our humanity. Because we didn't know God, we didn't understand the reality of relationships. We understood a whole lot of things, but we

didn't know God. And in that lack of knowledge of God—
or foolishness—we were darkened in every area of our
experience.

Many of us can look back to the time when God turned
on the lights in our lives and things began to make sense.
What was it exactly that turned on the lights? It was the
fact that we came to know Him. And when His light shone
into the darkness of our lives, we realized how utterly
dark it had been. "At one time," said the Apostle, "we too
were foolish." We were *darkened in our understanding.*

Not only were we darkened in our understanding, as
far as God is concerned, the Apostle said there was a time
when we were also disobedient. Now, we can be disobedient to God in a lot of ways. Simply reading the things that
come from God's Word and saying, "I don't believe that. I
don't buy that. I don't want anything to do with that. I am
simply going to ignore it," is being disobedient.

There are other people who will say, "Well, I believe
that's what God says, and I believe that's what I ought to
do, but quite frankly, there are other considerations, and I
don't want to do what God says; I much prefer to do what I
want to do." That's disobedience. There is also a sense in
which if I live in self-induced ignorance of what God says, I
am engaging in disobedience. The situation for a person
who doesn't know there is a Word of God is very different
from a person brought up in the North American continent
who has constant access to the Scriptures.

The particular situation of the person who is brought
up in a Christianized, westernized society, where he is
constantly exposed to the opportunity of reading the Word
of God and countless other books, Christian newspapers,
and periodicals, radio and television and still doesn't
bother to find out what God says—this person is living in
rank disobedience to what God says. And many of us can

look back to the time when we lived in self-induced ignorance of what God says. The net product of that was disobedience.

Now, the apostle Paul says to remind the people, and go on reminding the people, of what they used to be like. They used to live in such a way that the relationship was totally away from what it ought to have been. Their relationship to God was characterized by *disobedience to His truth,* and it was a darkening of their understanding.

In Relation to Self

Then Paul goes on to talk about relation to self. At one time we too were "deceived and enslaved by all kinds of passions and pleasures." Very interesting expressions here. *Deceived,* he says, *by misinformation.*

It would be easy for us to point out the time in our lives when God's truth burst into our consciousness and we began to understand how utterly wrong we had been. About what? About God; about everything. If I'm wrong about God, I'm wrong about the world. If I'm wrong about God, I'm wrong about humanity. If I'm wrong about God, I'm wrong about society. If I'm wrong about God, I'm wrong about reality, period. This is an overwhelming thought, but it happens to be true. If I am wrong about God, therefore, it means that I have developed a philosophy of life, and a life-style, that I think is right; but it is only when God shines into my life with the truth that I understand that I lived all those years deceived by error. What I thought was truth wasn't truth at all. What I thought was reality was fantasy. What I thought was the way to go was actually the way to destruction.

Scripture says, "There is a way that seems right to a man, but in the end it leads to death" (Prov. 14:12). Now, it is important to remind people that they, before they knew the Lord and acknowledged Christ as Savior and Lord, were living lives that, in relation to God, were characterized by darkness and disobedience. But as far as their own souls were concerned, their lives were characterized by utter deception. They had been sent all kinds of misinformation by the enemy of their souls and they got just about everything wrong.

Not infrequently, people say to me, "You know, I look at my life and I can't believe how many things I've gotten wrong. I look at my life and I can't believe how many wrong decisions I've made and how many situations I've gotten myself into that are an unbelievable mess." Why is that? It's because they were living their lives estranged from God and His truth. They were deceived by the enemy of their souls.

But notice that Paul says we not only lived lives where we were deceived by misinformation, but also were *dominated by self-centeredness* and self-interest. We were "deceived and enslaved by all kinds of passions and pleasures." People think that pleasure is great and they are all in favor of indulging in their own passions. And our present society advocates: "Get as much pleasure as you can; get as much gusto in life as you can; get it and live it with a great exuberance; if it feels good, do it." But what they don't tell us is what the Bible tells us: You live a life indulging in your passions where you are solely interested in your own pleasures, and you'll end up enslaved by your own passions and your own pleasures. That's what Paul is saying in Titus 3:3.

Scripture has something powerful to say to us that is in total contrast to what we are hearing all around us. Our society tells us that our passions are our own business and we should indulge in them. Our society tells us that the important thing is our pleasure and, if we can evaluate and find that something gives us pleasure, it must be right; therefore, it must be good. We tend to evaluate the whole of our experience by whether it gives us pleasure and whether it protects us from pain. Scripture says that if you go that way, indulging in your passions, being solely interested in your pleasures, you will end up utterly a slave to these things. It's important that we remind ourselves of this, because some of us can look back to times when our own greed was all that mattered. The tragic thing about that was, the more greedy we were, the more enslaved we became by our greed. We said to ourselves: "If I could just get a little bit more; if I could just have this, if I could just get out of this situation and get into that situation, I would be happy." The problem was that the more greedy we were, the more greedy we became; and the more we got, the less satisfied we were. In the end, we found ourselves captivated and dominated by things and circumstances instead of being liberated by them. We found ourselves exercising our own sensuality; we engaged in all kinds of sexual practices.

That's exactly what our society is telling us to do. They are insisting on sexual freedom. What they don't tell us is that if we go on engaging in what is euphemistically called sexual liberty, sexual freedom, alternate life-styles—whatever terms you want to use—we will end up a slave to our own passions, because we'll be totally consumed by the desire to satisfy ourselves. And if pleasure is the watchword of our lives, and we can only be happy when we are having a pleasurable experience, then we must never be bored and never engage in anything mundane or routine. If that's the way we're going to live, we're going to have to spend all our time, money and energy trying to avoid living in the real world and we become enslaved by our desire to escape reality.

That's where we used to be, folks—utterly dominated by our own desire for pleasure; utterly dominated by our insistence on the freedom to indulge in our own passions. And it was captivating, dominating, enslaving. We need to remind ourselves of where we used to be.

In Relation to Others

If my relationship to God is wrong, my relationship to myself will be wrong. And if my relationship to myself is wrong, then my relationship to other people is going to be all wrong, too. The person who is only interested in his own passions and pleasures doesn't make a very good husband. The person who is only interested in making sure that she's always happy and always looked after doesn't make a very good wife or mother. And the person who is totally self-absorbed makes a rotten employee and an even worse employer.

In other words, if I get myself wrong with God, I've got myself wrong with me, and I've got myself wrong with people all over the place. Look at what Paul goes on to say: "At one time we too were foolish, disobedient"— that's toward God—"deceived and enslaved by all kinds of passions and pleasures," that's as far as myself is concerned. Accordingly, he goes on, "We lived in malice and envy, being hated and hating one another." And how true many of us know this to be.

But, we have to look into our own lives and say that our relationships to others have been totally *distorted because our reactions* to them have not been what they ought to be. For example, we got married, and what were we interested in? Love? No. Passion. We got married and what were we concerned about? Commitment till death parts us? No. Our own pleasure is all we were interested in. We weren't interested in what God said about marriage. And we weren't interested in what God said about family.

If I lived my life making sure that I was always happy and my passions were always dealt with, I would become unbelievably malicious whenever another person wouldn't do as I wanted him to do. And this leads to hatred. That which passes for marriage today in our society is often a cruel parody of what marriage is intended to be. That which passes for families in many areas of society today are obscene caricatures of what family is supposed to be. How do we account this dichotomy? Because we are wrong as far as God is concerned; we're all wrong in our relationship with ourselves and, therefore, we cannot have proper relationships with one another. God tells us to go on reminding the people of what they used to be like. They are all wrong toward Him, all wrong toward themselves and all wrong toward others.

Can you look back to a time when you used to be like the person I just described? More importantly, can you now look at yourself and see the difference? That brings us to the second point. We are to go on reminding people not only of how they used to live, but how they were saved.

Reminding God's People How They Were Saved

But is one of my favorite words in the Bible; it's an important one. Always put a circle around it, because it is going to lead to a stark contrast to what has just been said. "We used to be this way at one time," Paul says, and then he goes on and says *but*.

There was a famous preacher in London, Dr. Martin

Lloyd-Jones, who was preaching through Romans and when he came to "But, God" I think he spent two months just sermonizing on that little phrase. I promise to be briefer!

"But when the kindness and love of God our Savior appeared, he saved us" (Titus 3:4-5). Why do we have to go on reminding ourselves of how we used to live? Because if we can go on reminding ourselves of how we used to live, we can start getting excited all over again about how God saved us. Let me, however, remind you first of two things.

Not All People Are God's People

It ought to be perfectly apparent to us that not all people are God's people because there are many in the world who cannot say what Paul says in verse 3, that we used to live this way. We used to be foolish and disobedient, deceived and enslaved. We used to live in malice and envy, being hated and hating one another. They can't say that. Why not? Because it isn't that they used to live that way. That's how they're living today.

Now, if we are living like that today, it would be nonsense for us to say, "But God saved me." How can I say God saved me if I'm still living as if I once lived in the past? If I'm still like that, then talking about being saved has a hollow sound. And this is important. Because while it is true to say that not all people are God's people, it is equally true to say that all God's people are saved people. What does that mean? It means that all God's people know that they're different from what they used to be.

All God's People Are Saved People

Now, of course, there are varying degrees in this differ-

If we can go on reminding
ourselves of how we used to
live, we can start getting
excited all over again about
how God saved us."

ence. There are some people who from their earliest days were brought up to know about the Lord and trusted what they knew about the Lord. But even those kinds of people have to be able to look back and say, "As I increasingly knew more of the Lord, as the Lord became increasingly real in my life, there's no question about it that there came a time in my life when things turned around." But probably the majority of us would have to say, "That was not my experience at all. My experience was such that I was disobedient to God. I lived in darkness as far as He was concerned. I was deceived by all the misinformation I got and I was dominated by my own self-centeredness, my own insistence on my own passions and pleasures. That's what I used to be like, but God intervened and saved me."

I'm not going to insist that you have to be able to point to a dramatic moment that in such and such a place and such and such a time God zapped you and changed you. What I'm going to say is this: If there's not evidence that God has changed you from what you were, then you need to take a good, long, hard look to see whether you were saved at all. And remember this: Not all people are God's people, but all God's people are saved people. He saved us.

First, *salvation is an act of God* as our Savior on our behalf. It is an act of God in mercy and loving kindness, not an action of man. Let me pull all that together by referring you to verses 4 and 5 again. "When the kindness and love of God our Savior appeared, he saved us, not because of righteous things we had done, but because of his mercy."

You can know God in many capacities: Father, Creator, Maker, Judge, Sustainer, Shepherd, and so on. But you must know Him as Savior, the One who intervened in your affairs and did something about your sins. He needs to be known as Savior, the One who moved into your life and changed you from what you were into what you are. Why did He do it? Because you deserved it? No. Because you merited it? No. Because it was your idea that He should do it? No. Why then did He do it? Because of lovingkindness and tender mercy and unmerited grace. Being changed from what you were into what you are is something that's attributable to God and to God alone.

We have been brainwashed into thinking that if anything is going to be achieved in our lives, we're going to have to do it ourselves. Well, get this straight if you've never gotten it straight before. You can't save yourself!

I remember some bored kids in a conference I had for teenagers in England some years ago. It was a typical English summer's day, with lots of *liquid* sunshine pouring out of the skies. We had about 500 kids there just hanging around and looking out the windows at the rain, bored to tears. I figured I had to do something, so I brought a bucket into the middle of the room. Then I said there was a pound note, a nice, crisp, green pound note, for the first kid who could stand in the bucket and lift himself off the ground. They thought that was the easiest pound they would ever earn in their lives. Kept them happy all afternoon, trying to earn their pound. And I've still got the pound, because you can't lift yourself off the ground standing in your own bucket. Neither can you save yourself. It's an act of God, who intervenes.

I earned my own pound that afternoon because, as a kid stood in the bucket, I leaned over and picked him up.

God in His loving kindness, tender mercy and capacity as Savior has moved into our lives and has done something for us we couldn't do for ourselves. Notice very carefully how Paul puts it in verse 4: "When the kindness and love of God our Savior appeared."

Remember the suspension bridge? Remember how God has appeared and how He will appear; and how that first dramatic appearance, or epiphany, was the epiphany of the appearance of grace, when God appeared in the person of Christ, like the dawn bursting onto the horizon and banishing the darkness? In Christ, He appeared. He lived on earth; He died on the cross; He rose again and returned to heaven. That is the first glorious appearing of God our Savior. In Christ's death and resurrection, God has done for us what we couldn't do for ourselves. He saved us. And God's people know what they used to be, but they also know they've been saved, through an act of God.

Second, *salvation is a fact.* "He saved us" (v. 5). Salvation is not something you sort of feel and then you don't feel. Salvation is something that is rooted in history. It is rooted in the appearance of God our Savior in the person of Christ. Jesus Christ really was born. He really did live. He really did die. He really did rise again. He demonstrated that He was the Son of God with authority by rising from the dead; and He proffers us salvation. Salvation is something that is factual. It can be shown to be factual and verifiable because it happened in history; it happened in time; it happened in space; it isn't just a theological concept; it isn't just a metaphysical experience. It is a factual thing. Christ appeared and died and rose again for our salvation. And we can go on reminding ourselves of this. God acted, and what He acted is a fact. We can be sure of it!

It was interesting to notice that the tense of the Greek that is used for "saved" in verse 5 is the aorist, which means it is an accomplished fact. He has specifically, definitely, incontrovertibly saved us. We are to go on reminding people of what they used to be, and go on reminding them that God saved them.

Third, *salvation is a pact* where God makes an agreement with us. He says to us, "If you will come in repentance and faith and allow me to do for you what you can't do for yourself; if you'll allow me to reach over and get hold of the bucket—that situation in which you find yourself, and allow me in Christ to pick you up when you can't pick yourself up, I promise to do it. I promise to save you from your sins. I promise to save you from your self-centeredness. I promise to save you from the consequence of your sins. I promise to save you from a lost eternity." We are supposed to go on reminding people of this.

I find a certain reluctance on many people's parts to say quite boldly, "I have been saved." I could never understand why. Are you reluctant to say that? Let me remind you, you are supposed to be able to say it because you know it. And you know it because God acted. He showed you that your salvation is a fact. He has made a pact with you that if you will come in repentance and faith, He will save you.

How can I know I'm saved? I can know initially because I take God at His word and believe and trust Him. But then I can know more definitely as time goes on because I continue to take Him at His word. And as I look back to where I used to be, do you know what I discover? "Wow! I've changed." Which isn't strictly true. It isn't that I have changed but that I have been changed. We have to go on reminding people what they used to be. We have to go on reminding people they are supposed to know they have been saved.

Reminding God's People How They Behave

It's one thing to say I've been saved. It's one thing to be

able to say God reached into my life and, in His glorious appearance, He did for me what I couldn't do for myself. But we've got to be able to substantiate it. And how do we do that? By the way we behave. Oh, let us stress this. God's people behave differently from those who are not God's people. That should be so obvious it ought not to be necessary to say. But we do need to go on reminding each other of this. Why? Because behaving differently from people who are not God's people is hard. And because it's hard, we forget.

Behaving differently means that we cannot indulge ourselves the way we used to do; and we want to indulge ourselves, so we carefully forget. Behaving differently means that I reject the things that many of my friends stand for. It means that I refuse to be what they insist I be; and that's going to mean some estrangement. So what do I do? I forget.

One of the greatest tragedies of the Christian Church in the North American continent is that we have millions of people who profess they have been saved, but show absolutely no evidence of it, because they insist on living the way the unsaved do. And many of the thinking people in the Church of Jesus Christ are saying that one of the great tragedies of the contemporary Church in North America is that we've got the manpower, we've got the womanpower, but we don't have the dynamic to change our society. Why is that?

If we want to be saved but don't want to be different, we won't change anything. The Apostle said, "Remind the people to be subject to rulers and authorities, to be obedient, to be ready to do whatever is good, to slander no one, to be peaceable and considerate, and to show true humility toward all men" (Titus 3:1,2).

Behavior in Terms of Authority

First of all, remind God's people that their behavior is supposed to be different in terms of authority. I hate to see a kid who professes to be a Christian argue with a referee. I really do. That turns me right off. He shows no respect for authority. I hate to see people who profess to be believers refusing to accept God-ordained authority in the fellowship of believers. That turns me right off. I really get perturbed about people who profess to be believers but have no readiness to accept the legal authorities of their society. They won't go along with the laws of the land; they resist them or break them as far as they can get away with it. That turns me right off. Let's face it: One of the ways we are going to show that we are saved is to show a respectful attitude toward authority.

There's a rotten attitude toward authority in our society today. You see it in sports; you see it in the way we drive our cars; you see it in just about every stratum of our society and every aspect of our lives. One of the ways that Christians show themselves different is by the respect they have for authority. Why? Because authority is God-ordained. It doesn't mean that we have to agree with the authority. It doesn't mean the authority is always right. But it does mean that God has ordained authority and we will respond to authority properly because we believe that all authority has its ultimate source in God Himself. Remind God's people to behave differently in terms of authority.

Behavior in Terms of Charity

Remind the people "to be ready to do whatever is good." Remind Christians in society that whenever they have the opportunity to do something good and kind and charitable, voluntarily they should be there on the front line. Look at the many charitable things that are going on in our society, the many attempts that are being made to assist people who are in deep need. Very often the remarkable thing is that we can't find believers who want to be involved in that kind of thing. Why? Because they haven't been prepared to be saved enough from their self-centeredness to get into volunteering to help somebody else. But what an impact it makes when believers begin to understand that saved people have a different attitude towards authority and saved people have a healthy attitude towards charity.

Behavior in Terms of Integrity

Remind the people "to slander no one, but to be peaceable and considerate, and to show true humility toward all men." As far as integrity is concerned, that means saying what is true and only speaking what is necessary. One of the most dangerous weapons we have in our considerable arsenal today is our tongue. What we say about people and what we say about each other is very often iniquitous, just not true, certainly not necessary and terribly damaging. I don't know how many hours I've spent in my pastorate trying to heal wounds that had been caused by somebody's tongue. And, quite frankly, most of the things that were said were certainly not necessary, and many of the things that were said just weren't true. Lack of integrity.

Behavior in Terms of Dignity

Try to be peaceable with people, try to be considerate to people and try to show true humility to people.

Jill caught the limousine to the airport in Tucson,

Arizona one day. The limousine hardly looked like a limousine; it was a beat-up old van. Jill and six men were the passengers, with a very glamorous little driver. Probably because the van was so beat up, the limousine company provided a glamorous driver. Anyway, the vehicle quit after a few blocks and the six men started raising cain because they wanted to get to their planes. The girl couldn't fix the van, so Jill asked, "What are we going to do?"

The driver said, "You're just going to have to flag down a cab."

Jill told the others she had an early flight—in fact hers was the first flight of all seven of them. A cab came along and three of the men piled in and took off. Another cab came along and the other three men piled in and took off. Jill was left there on her own, sitting inside the van.

I have no idea why these men acted with such discourtesy. Perhaps they felt so many women have screamed about equality for so long, they just decided to give it to them. Much can be said on both sides of the issue but one thing is not up for debate and that is that Christians do not behave like that—Christians feel a deep sense of dignity for all people. Christians are considerate people, courteous people, gentle people and meek people. In other words, Christians treat people with dignity. We need to keep reminding each other of that!

Questions for further study _____

1. Why is it important for Christians to be reminded of what they used to be like? Is the distance between where you are now and where you used to be vast or very small?

2. Considering where you used to be, describe your spiritual growth in the following areas:
   —In relation to God.
   —In relation to yourself.
   —In relation to others.
3. Explain the author's words: Not all people are God's people, but all God's people are saved people.
4. How should we Christians be able to substantiate our salvation? God's people behave differently from those who are not His people. Does your behavior in the following areas serve to substantiate your salvation and relationship to God:
   —In your home?
   —In your church?
   —In your community?
   —In your workplace?

CHAPTER SEVEN

Motivating God's People

I. Underscoring what is important

A. Where salvation originates

1. The grace of God
2. Appearing of Jesus Christ
3. Outpouring of the Holy Spirit

B. What salvation incorporates

1. Washing of rebirth
2. Renewal by the Holy Spirit
3. Justification by grace
4. Heirs of eternal life

C. What salvation relates

II. Understanding what is significant

A. Theology of Christianity based on grace

B. Ethics of Christianity built on gratitude

III. Undertaking what is necessary

A. Devotion to what is good

B. Desiring what is excellent

Titus 3:5-8

He saved us through the washing of rebirth and renewal by the Holy Spirit, whom he poured out on us generously through Jesus Christ our Savior, so that, having been justified by his grace, we might become heirs having the hope of eternal life. This is a trustworthy saying. And I want you to stress these things, so that those who have trusted in God may be careful to devote themselves to doing what is good. These things are excellent and profitable for everyone.

One of the great themes that occurs over and over again in this brief Epistle is that those who are believers behave in a specific and special way. And one of the unique aspects of the behavior of believers is that they are involved in actions that demonstrate their relationship to the Lord, actions that are to a great extent connected to the way they treat people. We find a constant emphasis that if you are a believer you are committed in your society to living a life of doing that which is good.

One of the problems we have in religious experience, however, is the matter of motivation. It's really difficult for some people to get around to being spiritually motivated. There are a number of reasons for this. One is that there are so many demands on our time and resources that as we juggle all these things we have a problem keeping all our balls in the air. Often the ball that gets dropped is the involvement in our religious or spiritual experience. Now, this is not specifically true for all people. For instance, there are some people who are unbelievably devoted to religious activity. They are phenomenally motivated in this particular area, devoting their whole lives to it. They will give up everything, making vows and commitments, where it becomes obvious that absolutely nothing else matters except their spiritual experience. But if you evaluate their motivation, often you discover the reason for that assiduous motivation, determination and overwhelming devotion is that they are working on the assumption that if they are devoted enough, busy enough and motivated enough, then hopefully, everything will work out in the end and they will be saved; they will come into an experience of the living God.

In other words, there are a lot of people who are highly motivated in the religious realm, hoping they will be saved, as a reward.

Now, of course, the problem with this motivation is that Scripture tells us repeatedly that salvation is not a reward for a highly motivated or a highly devoted life. Over and over again, we see in Scripture, not least in the Epistle to Titus, that the principle of salvation is not that God saves us because of the righteous things we have done. On the contrary, the righteous things we have done are, in God's sight, "like filthy rags" (Isa. 64:6). They are not going to earn the reward of salvation.

Accordingly, Christian leaders have a big problem, because if people have a hard time being motivated religiously speaking—and then only for a reward—and you take away the possibility of reward, how on earth are you going to keep them involved? How are you going to get them motivated? How are you going to get them inspired to do anything at all? This is one of the great problems confronting the Christian Church today.

Now, everybody in the pastorate is aware of this problem. That's why you find a variety of methodology to motivate people, who know they are not going to be saved because of what they do, and, therefore, are not particularly interested in doing anything at all.

Some preachers share their great burden and plead with people. Often the pleading works with one or two rather sensitive souls, but on the whole, it doesn't make any difference at all.

Another approach is to threaten: "I'm going to do this if you don't do this," and people simply accept the threats and do as they want to anyway; threats don't make any difference. Another is to challenge: "I challenge you to do certain things." It's amazing how, if you challenge people long enough, they become totally inoculated against it.

So, pleading doesn't work. Threatening doesn't work. Challenging doesn't work. Offering an ultimatum doesn't work. Offering rewards only works so long. What on earth, then, can we do to get people motivated?

Granted, a lot of people in the church will be motivated to do things if they think they can be saved because of their works. But what on earth can you do with people who have *been* saved by grace and mercy and the lovingkindness of God? How are we going to get them to clean up their act? The answer to that is one of the most important we can ever deal with in Scripture. And that is what Paul does here: He deals with how Titus is to motivate the people in Crete to live lives of goodness, challenge, commitment and involvement. That's how the Christian Church is called to live.

Motivation Includes Underscoring What Is Important

First of all, we have to notice that Paul's motivating factor, basically, as far as his ministry is concerned, is teaching. He is constantly underscoring the spiritual truths that are important. It seems to me that over and over again the apostle Paul is not so much pleading or threatening, or challenging people, as he is teaching them. And, he seems to have tremendous confidence that when people are properly and adequately taught there will be an assimilation of truth, which will become a fuel of motivation in their lifestyles. Motivating includes underscoring what is important.

Where Salvation Originates

You'll notice that the Apostle is very careful to go on stressing, almost ad nauseam, that salvation does not originate with man or is the product of human activity, but salvation originates with God.

You know, we could go on saying that forever. Salvation originates with God, not with man. We can insist that salvation is by grace and faith alone, and not of righteous works. Yet, between Sundays, we can sit and talk with people who still think that salvation originates with them and is a product of their good living.

Now, even as I've written this exposition of the Word of God as found in Titus, I realize how deep-rooted the idea is that salvation originates with man and is the product of the way we live. We have to go on stressing that this is one of the most fundamental errors in human thinking; it is rooted in human pride! We believe that we are the circumference of all things. Deep down, we really believe that we have the solution to all things and that somehow or another everything depends on us. Even our spiritual relationship is fundamentally dependent upon us doing things right so that God can respond.

But salvation, Scripture tells us, originates with *the grace of God.* Titus 3:7 states categorically we are justified by His grace. Verse 4 tells us that "the kindness and love of God our Savior appeared" so that He might save us "because of his mercy." If you experience salvation, it is totally attributable to the grace, mercy and lovingkindness of God. It started there because God wanted to give to you what you didn't deserve. I hope, trust and long to believe that you have grasped this, because it is utterly fundamental to the uniqueness of Christianity.

Second, salvation, having originated with the grace of God, also *appears in the person of Jesus Christ.* Remember in verse 6, speaking of our Lord Jesus, Paul says, "He poured out on us generously through Jesus Christ our Savior" the Holy Spirit. Remember the expression in Titus 2:13 there was a glorious appearing of our Lord Jesus. Remember our salvation, originating with the grace of God, is made available to us exclusively in our Lord Jesus Christ.

Now, it's remarkable there are still people in our churches who think they can be saved in all kinds of different ways, that it doesn't really matter what you believe, as long as you are sincere. And there are people who have heard the preaching of the Word of God for weeks and months, some of them for years, and the fact of salvation still has not clicked. That is why people aren't interested in missions. They still have the idea it doesn't matter about those who know nothing of Christ; they're not really lost. They don't see why it's important that people should go and give of themselves to take the message of Christ to those who have never heard. They don't think it's important, because they don't seem to be prepared to accept the fact that Scripture tells us that salvation is available in Jesus Christ exclusively; there is salvation in none other.

Remember this: If it's true that our salvation originates with the grace of God, and is made available to us exclusively in the person of Jesus Christ, it means that we are totally locked in to God graciously making Christ available to us, and not to us alone, but to the whole world.

Third, our salvation originates in *the outpouring of the Holy Spirit.* Now, we have pointed out in this book that salvation comes in different tenses. There is the past tense in which we can say we "have been saved." There's the future tense in which we look forward with confidence and say we "will be saved." And there is the present tense in which we can look at our daily experience and say we "are being saved." In all these dimensions the Holy Spirit is at work.

Do you know why you were saved? You were saved because the grace of God—an attitude of God—took the initiative and provided Christ for you, a Christ you couldn't provide for yourself. Do you know how you came to understand and respond to the message of Christ? It was because the Spirit of God opened your blind eyes, touched your hard hearts, moved your chloroformed consciences and began to allow you to understand the depth of your own sin and the wonder of Christ's glory. Do you know how it is that you can look back on your past and say, "I used to be like that but I'm not anymore: There has been a change or transformation in my life"? It is because the Holy Spirit who opened your eyes has now come into your heart and is slowly transforming you into the image of Christ. It was the work of the Holy Spirit. You didn't open your eyes. It wasn't through your remarkable capabilities. It wasn't through your great rational intelligence that you

You were saved because the grace of God . . . took the initiative and provided Christ for you, a Christ you couldn't provide for yourself."

were able to grasp the immensity of truth. It was the work
of the Holy Spirit—inspiring Scripture, inspiring preacher
and witness, working in your own heart bringing conviction and understanding—that brought you to salvation.

If we're going to motivate people properly in the Christian Church, we have to do it by getting them to understand the things that are important. Of prime importance
is that your salvation originated with the grace of God
through the appearing of Christ in the outpouring of the
Holy Spirit. It wasn't you who did it, and it wasn't I who did
it. It was all of grace. It was all of mercy. It was all of divine
initiative. That has to be fundamental in our understanding.

What Salvation Incorporates

We've got to underscore what salvation incorporates.

First of all, in verse 5, Paul talks about the *washing of
rebirth*. This expression immediately suggests two things
to me. First of all, the word *washing* obviously speaks of
the necessity of cleansing from defilement. Rebirth speaks
immediately of the opportunity for a fresh beginning. Now,
theologians have had a marvelous time disagreeing over
this expression. We are not going to get into the area of
disagreement, but will concentrate on the thrust of the
passage to help us understand how to motivate God's people. And the answer is by making sure they understand
the things that are important.

One of the important things is that when we are saved,
we have been cleansed from past defilement and introduced into an experience where we have the priceless
privilege of a fresh beginning. Now, there are some who
rejoice in this. There are people who are rather like the
sinful woman who came to our Lord Jesus, when He was

at the banquet table, and put the precious ointment on His feet, weeping and wiping her tears from His feet with her hair. And when the people criticized her for such unbecoming behavior, our Lord Jesus said: "Her many sins have been forgiven—for she loved much" (Luke 7:47).

There are people like that. I meet them week after week. They tell me of their sordid past, the depth of sin they had gotten into and the trail of wreckage it has left. They look back over their experiences and feel so guilty. And so they should. But then they say, "The wonderful thing that happened is that God in His grace sent Jesus to appear on my behalf and the Holy Spirit moved in my life and touched me and revealed the depth of my sin and the wonder of Christ's redemption. And He enabled me to respond to Him, and now I know that my sins have been cleansed. Though my sins were scarlet, they have become as white as snow. Though they were red like crimson, they are as white as wool" (see Isa. 1:18).

One of the great recurring themes in many people's lives is, "I know what I was like and I know I've been cleansed. I know what I was like and I know it has all been blotted out and I am so grateful."

I've observed that often the people who understand that salvation means a washing, a cleansing, a blotting out of their past are people who are the most highly motivated in Christian service. Those who have been forgiven much, more often than not, are the ones who love much. Those who understand the depth of their sin are the ones who get excited about the wonder of their cleansing. They are so excited about it they want to take every opportunity to express thanksgiving.

The washing of rebirth also speaks of a new beginning. The theme of being born again, regeneration—or the literal word here is a new genesis, a new beginning—is found in many parts of Scripture. And it's a delightful theme.

There are many people who talk about their past; they'll look at their lives often with a note of despair. They wonder how on earth anything could have ever come out of their lives. But the great message of the Christian gospel is that God is prepared to move into the dirtiest life and clean it up. He is prepared to move into the most broken life and give it a new genesis. And the wonder of this new beginning is that Christ becomes our Savior and Lord. God gives us a new beginning in that the Holy Spirit pours out generously upon us and becomes the dynamic of a whole new experience.

Think of how new a beginning this is. Up until that time you steered your own ship, you paddled your own canoe. Up until that time you went down the rapids of society and came up against the rocks and the boulders; you were swamped and bruised and were sinking. But then something dramatic happened. You turned the control of your canoe over to the Lord, a mighty Holy Spirit who was able to get into the situation and take charge. That's the new beginning.

The apostle Paul says it is imperative that we stress these things to people so they can understand that salvation incorporates cleansing from past defilements and the opportunity for a fresh beginning.

Now then, some of you are still saying, "Well, what's the controversy in all this?" The controversy stems from the word *washing*. Many commentators—probably most commentators—say this means that through baptism you are regenerated and through baptism you have this renewal.

One branch of Christendom interprets it as follows: If a person goes through the experience of baptism, that automatically—almost in a mechanical sense—ensures that the person is regenerated and renewed. Let me take this to its most extreme position. When Jill was about to produce our third child, Peter, she was having all kinds of problems. Peter wasn't too enthusiastic about coming into this cold world. He has always been very fond of his own comforts, and we should have realized way back then what he was going to be like. He was in no hurry at all. He was laid-back then; he is laid-back now. Eventually, however, he arrived on the scene, but only after numerous false alarms and much consternation on the part of those who were caring for Jill and the unborn baby.

There was a nurse in the hospital who was looking after Jill. She said to me, "Do you realize that there is a very real possibility that this baby might die?"

And I answered, "Yes, I fully realize that is a possibility."

"Well," she said, "what steps have you taken to baptize this baby the moment it is born?"

I said, "None whatsoever."

She said, "I think you are grossly out of order. I cannot believe that anybody would have such an attitude, and I insist that you make arrangements for somebody to be here so that the moment that baby is born, it may be baptized."

So I said, "Why?"

"Because if the baby is not baptized and dies, the baby will go to hell."

So I said, "But if the baby is baptized what will happen?"

"He'll go to heaven."

"In other words," I said, "he's going to be saved by baptism?"

She said, "Exactly."

And I said, "Well, madam, with all due respect, you're exactly wrong."

"No, you're exactly wrong." And she went on, "I'm going to tell you something. If you don't make arrangements to have that baby baptized, I personally will baptize the baby myself."

And I said, "God bless you. Go right ahead. Go right ahead."

"Well," she said, "that is not really what you ought to do. You ought to have a minister come in and do it."

Now, this lady was deeply sincere—and I know I'm on delicate grounds here. She could have appealed, if she'd known the Bible—which she didn't—to Titus 3:5 and other similar verses. And she could have said, "Listen. It is through the washing that rebirth and renewal takes place. It is through baptism."

The thing we've got to point out, however, is this: Nowhere does Scripture teach that regeneration, renewal and reconciliation to God are the results of a mechanical application of a rite. Rather, Scripture teaches that regeneration and renewal are the result of people responding in faith to the grace of God.

Now then, sometimes you'll find that all God does is spoken of as being related to faith, and other times you'll find it is related to baptism. In other words, what the Scripture is saying is this: People are regenerated and renewed through faith in the grace of God, and incorporated in this whole act of faith is the act of baptism. Not that baptism, in an automatic, mechanical sense, will produce salvation without faith, but that faith will also require a person to take a stand as far as his relationship with Christ is concerned, and part of that stand is experiencing baptism.

I may be writing to some who think you can be saved

Scripture teaches that regeneration and renewal are the result of people responding in faith to the grace of God."

through baptism alone. But you are overlooking the whole thrust of this passage that says that we are justified by grace, and it is those who believe in God who are saved.

Second, if you are a believer, but have not recognized the significance of baptism, you need to take another hard look at it. Because if you have not in one mode or another, experienced baptism, this is something that ought to be done.

Now, of course, another side of the argument says that the washing does not refer to baptism at all, but rather to the ministry of the Word of God. And, of course, you can get into a study of that if you so desire.

What does salvation incorporate? The washing of rebirth, cleansing from past defilement, and an opportunity for a fresh beginning, not through the mechanical application of some rite of the Church, but through the grace of God to which we respond in faith. Signed and sealed by baptism.

Second, also in verse 5, salvation incorporates *renewal by the Holy Spirit.* This idea of renewal is another beautiful theme in Scripture. For instance, we are told in Colossians 3:10 that when we come to faith in Christ, we are made a new person. The old person is gone; the new person has been made in the image of Christ. We are told in Romans 12:2 that we have a new mind that is constantly being renewed. And we are told in 2 Corinthians 4, that even though our outward body is wasting away—that means our hair is dropping out, our skin is getting all kinds of wrinkles, and whatever we do to make it appear that this is not the case, it is the case—our inner man is being renewed. What does this mean?

It means that when I come to faith in Christ, God in His grace through Christ, pouring out the Holy Spirit into my life, gives me the opportunity to be a new person. He will draw the drapes on the old person. The old person, as Paul says in Romans 6:4, has been buried with Christ in baptism. We died with Christ in order that we might be raised into newness of life with Christ.

This is one of the most exciting things you can tell people, particularly those who would love to be able to walk away from their past, to feel that God can renew them and give them the opportunity to do something positive after having had a long career at that which is negative. That is exactly what he is saying here: It is possible for us to be renewed by the Holy Spirit, to be made a new man, to be able to walk away from the old man, to have a new mind—which means a new attitude—and to have this attitude being constantly renewed. And even though outwardly we are fading away, inwardly there is that renewal, that refreshing, that strengthening. The older we get, the more refreshing and the more renewed we become. That's what God does in salvation, if we respond in faith to His grace.

Then, third, in verse 7 Paul talks about being *justified by His grace*. The word *justified* is related to the word *righteousness*. The Bible teaches the righteousness of God, which means, among other things, that He is always right.

Now, in sharp contrast to the sinlessness of the always-rightness of God, man is sinful and has done things that are unrighteous. And the big human dilemma is, how can an unrighteous man find his way into the presence of a righteous God? The answer is only through the justification that stems from the grace of God.

What is justification? Justification means literally that God declares me right with Him. It's a legal term. It's like I'm on trial and God is sitting on the bench; He is my judge. The charge is made against me—what I've been; what I've done. The whole sordid thing is there. All the evidence comes out. It is irrefutable—there's not a thing I can do about it. There I am before a holy, absolutely just God, and He knows everything about me. He hears all there is to hear about me and then He pronounces the verdict, which is a foregone conclusion: Guilty. Of course, I'm guilty before the eyes of a righteous God.

What then can I do? I can stand there and simply admit my guilt. I can bring out the petty little things I have done in my religious observance in my half-hearted "good life." But it has a hollow sound in the courtroom of God, who listens to it all and pronounces me guilty nevertheless. And I know it is true; I am guilty.

God sentences me, but then He does the most remarkable thing. He takes off His robe of office, steps down and Himself pays the fine. He offers me that which I cannot handle myself. And having offered me the payment for the fine, He then goes back to the bench, puts on His robes, and declares something that is music to my ears: "This person before me is utterly unrighteous; I the righteous God have found him guilty. The judgment has been passed; but the penalty has been paid. I paid it myself and, therefore, I, the righteous judge, proclaim him free. I proclaim him without any further obligation before me. I, the righteous God, declare him righteous-justified."

All of you come to that court and say, "Whew, what a good thing I joined the church and started tithing when I was 45. Wow, if I hadn't started tithing, I'd never have made it up here to heaven. What a good thing I was kind to my aged mother when she was 83. That brought me here." No, you won't say any of that. What will you say? You will walk out of that courtroom and say, "I'm utterly unrighteous before a righteous God. But that righteous God rightly found me guilty; paid the penalty Himself in His precious Son, our Lord Jesus; offered me that which I couldn't earn for myself, and by faith I took it. He donned His robes of office again, and He, the righteous judge, declared me righteous." Why? Grace! And don't ever forget it.

The apostle Paul, having explained all this in the Epistle to the Romans, asks, "Where then do we have any grounds for boasting?" And I love his response. Boasting, he said, "Is excluded" (Rom. 3:27). One of the nice things about heaven is that nobody will be bragging at all because there will be nobody there who has anything to brag about. The only people in heaven will be those who have been justified freely by His grace; who have been regenerated; who have been renewed and made *heirs of eternal life.*

What Salvation Relates

We have been applying this last point all the way through. Grace makes salvation available. The empty hand of repentant faith makes salvation actual, and those who are thus justified, out of gratitude are deeply motivated to honor their Savior and Lord.

Motivation Includes Understanding What Is Significant

The theology of Christianity is based on grace. If you don't understand this, go back and read it again. Check every reference. Study the Word of God and say, "God, make this make sense, please." And He'll say, "Delighted. I'll be happy to do that."

While the theology of Christianity is based on grace, *the ethics of Christianity are built on gratitude.* In other words, I've got my theology straight, I understand how salvation works and how I became rightly related with God. But once I've done that, there is an ethical demand upon me. I'm supposed to behave a certain way now that I'm a believer. I ought to do some things, and ought not to do other things. This is what we call the ethics of Christianity. How can we get people to do what they should? How can we get people to stop doing what they should not do? Answer: We can do it when people are so caught up in the theology of grace that they grasp the ethics of gratitude. Or, to put it simply: When I'm overwhelmed with the goodness and unmerited favor of God, I will have, born in my heart, an overwhelming sense of gratitude, and I will exhibit it by being what God wants me to be. Therein lies the purest motivation for the Christian.

You can threaten them as long as you like. You can plead with them as much as you want. You can challenge them till you're blue in the face. But I have come to the conviction that, in the long run, while all these things may well have their valid place in terms of motivation, the primary motivation is that people begin to understand that it is the grace of God alone that brings salvation, and it is gratitude to God that motivates them to live as they should.

That's why when people come to me and talk about their Christian motivation, I usually, to their surprise, go back to the beginning and try to make sure that they understand the simple message of the grace of God. When I remember where I was until God in His grace touched me, I have no difficulty recognizing where people are and that motivates me towards them.

I hear people talking about burnout. I've heard of burned-out nurses, burned-out teachers and even burned-out preachers! Perhaps we need to have a union for preachers! We could call it UBOP: Union of Burned-Out

Preachers. We've got bebop, now UBOP. Wouldn't that be great? I'm not serious of course!

I get alarmed when I hear about burned-out preachers, because it seems to me that any preacher who understands the grace of God, and remembers where he used to be, should have adequate resources of grace to keep him encouraged and enabled for the ministry of grace. Of course there are other considerations that need to be taken into account, but generally speaking an adequate grasp of grace should keep all of us on the job.

Motivation Includes Undertaking What Is Necessary

"This is a trustworthy saying. And I want you to stress these things, so that those who have trusted in God may be careful to devote themselves to doing what is good. These things are excellent and profitable for everyone" (Titus 3:8). As we think in terms of motivating people in the Christian Church, we're not thinking so much of pleading; we're not thinking so much of challenging. We're thinking primarily of teaching. Teaching people, underscoring the things that are important in such a way that the people understand what is significant so that eventually they will undertake what is necessary. And what is necessary? An utter *devotion to what is good*. A tremendous *desire for what is excellent* before God.

It is up to the individual believer to discover in the context of the fellowship of believers the good works for which he was redeemed and then to do them wholeheartedly as unto the Lord. This honors God, blesses those who are ministered to and wonderfully enriches the involved believer.

Questions for further study _____

1. What is one of the great problems confronting the Christian Church today? Is there evidence of this problem in your local church?
2. Are you clear on where your salvation originates? Review Titus 3:5-7. Are there people you know who are unclear about the source of their salvation? What steps could you take to help them understand this vital aspect of the Christian life?
3. The author asks two very important questions in this chapter. First, do you know why you were saved, and, second, do you know how you came to understand and respond to the message of Christ? It would be wise to go back over this section and be sure you understand this concept clearly.
4. What does the term *washing of rebirth* mean to you?

CHAPTER EIGHT

Warning God's People

I. Division in the church cannot be accepted

A. Anatomy of a division

1. Raising of an issue
2. Introduction of an emphasis
3. Reaction of the people
4. Escalation of the situation

B. Analysis of a division

1. Differences are inevitable
2. Difficulties are probable
3. Divisions are possible

C. The anathema of a division

1. The Body suffers amputation
2. Cause of Christ suffers misrepresentation
3. Disciples of Christ suffer humiliation

II. Discipline in the church must not be avoided

A. When is discipline necessary?

1. When people disrupt the building of the Body
2. When practices corrupt the life of the Body
3. When problems interrupt the ministry of the Body

B. How is discipline administered?

1. The people concerned are approached
2. The people are approached again
3. The people concerned are disciplined

Titus 3:8-15

I want you to stress these things, so that those who have trusted in God may be careful to devote themselves to doing what is good. These things are excellent and profitable for everyone. But avoid foolish controversies and genealogies and arguments and quarrels about the law, because these are unprofitable and useless. Warn a divisive person once, and then warn him a second time. After that, have nothing to do with him. You may be sure that such a man is warped and sinful; he is self-condemned. As soon as I send Artemas or Tychicus to you, do your best to come to me at Nicopolis, because I have decided to winter there. Do everything you can to help Zenas the lawyer and Apollos on their way and see that they have everything they need. Our people must learn to devote themselves to doing what is good, in order that they may provide for daily necessities and not live unproductive lives. Everyone with me sends you greetings. Greet those who love us in the faith. Grace be with you all.

This is a very small letter the apostle Paul writes to his fellow worker Titus. The two of them had been ministering together on the Island of Crete. They had moved among the pagan peoples, preached the gospel, and as a result, many came to know Christ personally and intimately.

But that was not the end of their work. That was only the beginning of their work. And as Paul moved on he told Titus to remain in Crete, the objective being that he gather together all these individuals who had come to a knowledge of Christ and establish churches. He was to move into all the towns and cities of Crete and finish the work that had been started. In particular, in order that the churches might become established, Titus was called to ordain elders so that they could properly oversee and lead the work, and so the people could be carefully taught.

It is important that we recognize the place of the local church in the economy of God. Viewed from the human point of view, the local church is a gathering of people who have in common their relationship to the Lord Jesus. And as we have seen in this Epistle, viewed from the divine perspective, the local church is called God's very own people.

There's something special about a local church as far as society is concerned, because it is a model of what society is supposed to be when it operates under divine principles. But there is something very special about the local church as far as God is concerned. For the local church is, in the view of God, a group of people who are known uniquely and distinctively in their geographic location as God's very own people.

Because you have the privilege in your local church of being God's very own people, you also have a corresponding responsibility. And that is you should not only live individually in such a way that people know you belong to the Lord Jesus, but you should also live corporately as His children. Not only is our world going to look at the behavior of individuals to get a feel for who Christ is, but our world can quite legitimately look at a corporate group of people, a body of believers, in order that they might also see what it is that is different about a Christian. And let's face it, a person who is not a believer wants to know if Christian theology is for real. A person who is not a believer wants to know what it is that makes believers so different.

One of the best ways to show the difference is by pointing to the unique society called the local church or God's very own people and then by pointing out how they behave corporately in a way that is different from other groups of people in our society. What a pressing responsibility it is, not only to be a believer, but to be a member of the local fellowship, a member of the Church of Christ.

Now, with all that in mind, we come to a rather solemn final word from the apostle Paul. We're not going to look into the personal greetings to the individuals he mentions here and the particular significance of them, but we are going to look into the very serious things the apostle Paul says, which I have entitled "Warning God's People."

Warning—Division in the Church Not Accepted

Why do we need to warn God's people? Because it is very easy for individual Christians and for the corporate Body of Christ to behave in a way that is incompatible with a profession of faith in Christ. And, accordingly, we need to be constantly warned and reminded of what is reasonably expected of behavior in the fellowship. In this chapter we are going to talk about Paul's warning that division in the church cannot be accepted. Look at verse 10: "Warn a divisive person once, and then warn him a second time. After that, have nothing to do with him." And if you're not sure what that means, will this help: strike one; strike two; you're out! Now, that's perhaps a rather crude way of

putting it, but the apostle Paul speaks so forcibly, so seriously, so solemnly about division in the Church of Jesus
Christ that he says it's totally unacceptable.

I think one of the weaknesses of the Church in the contemporary setting is that we have become soft in the
whole area of division. We have not realized how serious it
is for people who profess to be a Body of believers to live
in such a way that it is perfectly obvious they are not a
Body. And often we simply paint over the cracks; we
whitewash the situation, hoping it will go away; or we pre-
tend it never came about. As a result, in many instances,
the Church of Jesus Christ loses her credibility. That's why
we need to read carefully what the Apostle is saying here.

The Anatomy of a Division

What do we mean by a division in the Church and how
does it come about? Well, you'll notice that, first of all,
Paul says in verse 9, that Titus and the people to whom he
is ministering are to "avoid foolish controversies."

The raising of an issue. The Greek word for controversy has its roots in the word for "to seek." I have a feeling that most controversies start because people are interested enough in a topic to seek out what is really involved.
They get involved and start studying it with increasing
intensity. Then they bump up against somebody who
doesn't necessarily see eye-to-eye with them, and they
start debating.

This Greek word *controversy* starts off initially with the
idea of "to seek," then eventually comes to mean "to
debate." But then there is a particular usage of the word in
the New Testament. The word that started out "to seek"
and then became "debate" eventually degenerates into
"controversy." Now, the apostle Paul is talking specifically

about controversies here in Titus. Notice the adjective he uses to describe them. He talks about "foolish controversies."

People seek to know the truth of a matter; then other people will see different sides of it, and inevitably this results in debates and discussions. However, these discussions and debates can become controversial. When those controversies become "foolish controversies," you have the seeds of a division. And the apostle Paul says to watch it very carefully, indeed. Just to encourage you, the word *foolish* in the Greek is the word from which we get moron. In other words, be very careful. People who are seeking to know things in certain areas can become so intensely involved and get into such discussion and debate that it can degenerate into a controversy. And the controversy can become so bad that it might only adequately be described as moronic controversy.

The introduction of an emphasis. "Avoid foolish controversies and genealogies." When Paul wrote to Timothy in Ephesus, as well as to Titus in Crete, he pointed out that they were going to have trouble with what he calls in another place "endless genealogies." What were they? Well, there were certain teachers who would take some of the genealogies of the Old Testament and decide they weren't complete enough. So they began to fill in the cracks—or what they thought were cracks—with all kinds of myths. As a result, they would produce the most fanciful ideas imaginable; then they would spend all their time discussing and debating the particular things that were of interest to them.

I don't know if you have noticed this, but in the Church of Jesus Christ, it is so easy to get interested in an *emphasis.* Always remember that an emphasis unrelated to the corresponding emphasis of Scripture is the breeding

Always remember than an emphasis unrelated to the corresponding emphasis of Scripture is the breeding ground for a heresy."

ground for a heresy. One of the problems we have in our contemporary church is that emphases become fads. It has been suggested that perhaps one of the most chronic ills of the contemporary church in North America at the present time is "fadism." It isn't that we're into endless genealogies, but it is that we're not satisfied with what Scripture says, so we have to fill in what we feel it should have said, and build up and emphasize the whole thing and get gung ho about it. We push it to such lengths that we can no longer substantiate it from Scripture. As a result, we begin to muddy the waters. Now, this kind of a situation, coupled with foolish controversies, can be ecclesiastical dynamite. It can be the beginning of a division in the church.

The reaction of the people. "Avoid foolish controversies and genealogies and arguments." The word *argument* here is translated "strife" in other parts of the Scripture—people just getting upset; people in the Church of Jesus Christ getting into these emphases, into these positions, into these situations, and getting thoroughly upset about it. Instead of having harmony in the church, instead of really being united in being what they are called to be, people get themselves absorbed with the issues. Soon you begin to sense uneasiness.

Now, the Apostle says to watch out for this. He gives us an example of this kind of thing in 1 Corinthians 3:1-3 as he addresses the church in Corinth, which was a model of what a church should *not* be. He said, "I could not address you as spiritual but as worldly—mere infants in Christ. I gave you milk, not solid food, for you were not ready for it. Indeed, you are still not ready. You are still worldly. For since there is jealousy and quarreling among you, are you not worldly? Are you not acting like mere men? For when one says, 'I follow Paul,' and another 'I follow Apollos,' are you not mere men." What Paul is saying is this: In the Church of Jesus Christ, we can respond to situations in a spiritually immature way, a "worldly way;" that is, a purely secular reaction to a spiritual situation.

Now, he says, if we respond to these emphases or particular concerns in a secular way or in an inadequate spiritual way, the result is going to be all kinds of upset and strife. And this, of course, showed itself particularly in the church of Corinth. Because the people, instead of addressing the problems they were confronting, began to attack the people identified with the problems. One of the surest signs that the church is having difficulty is when personalities related to a problem rather than the problem become attacked.

Now, this is what was happening in the church of Corinth, in the church of Ephesus and in the church of Crete. It should come as no surprise if it therefore happens in the church today, anywhere on the face of God's earth. Remember, these attacks are the anatomy of a division.

The escalation of the situation. Paul, then, uses an even stronger word. He says you have "foolish controversies and genealogies and arguments and quarrels about the law." The word *quarrel* is simply the word for "fight." I don't know why he just didn't say fight. A good, old knock-down-drag-out church fight. And fight is related to the word for sword. When the swords are drawn, it is an utter disgrace to the Church of Jesus Christ.

So, Paul says to warn the people who may be involved in this kind of a situation. Division in the Church is totally unacceptable.

Analysis of a Division

Let's just back up a little bit and see how these fights come about. There are three words to notice particularly. The first word is *difference*. The second is *difficulty*. And the third is *division*. I believe with all my heart that differences are inevitable in the Church of Jesus Christ. Because differences are inevitable, difficulties are probable. If there are differences in a group of people then there is a high probability they will run into difficulties.

But let's take it a step further. If difficulties over differences are probable in the Church of Jesus Christ, then divisions are possible. What is a division? A division is a difficulty handled improperly. You say, "Well, let's get rid of all the difficulties." How are you going to do that? I'll tell you. Get rid of all the people. If you don't want the probability of difficulty and if you don't want the possibility of division, there's only one way to handle it, and that is to empty the church of people.

But, you see, we can't do that. Instead, let's stick with the people. Let's accept that there will be differences; there will be difficulties. But let's make absolutely certain that in the differences and the difficulties, division is never allowed to raise its ugly head. That is basically what Paul is saying.

Differences are inevitable. Why will there be differences in the Church of Jesus Christ?

First, there are differences, wide differences, in *scriptural knowledge.* In the Church of Jesus Christ some people will speak with tremendous authority on a subject and never even crack a Bible. But that doesn't stop them from speaking their mind on it; even though their mind is singularly unenlightened as far as scriptural truth is concerned.

On the other hand, you'll find some people who have studied very carefully and very assiduously. They will then address a situation from a totally different perspective. However, that doesn't mean that the person who studied

Scripture has all the answers and is always right. Neither does it mean that the person who has not studied Scripture doesn't have any answers and is always wrong. But what Paul points out is this: When you have differences in scriptural knowledge, you have people addressing an issue from totally different vantage points. Let's face it, there are some people who don't know much about the Bible, but they are gifted with good old common sense.

Let's thank God for people who have common sense. It would be marvelous if these people with common sense could take the trouble to find out what God says in His Word.

It is equally probable that you will come across people who have really studied God's Word, but they haven't brought much common sense to bear on it. Perhaps they have studied one aspect of God's Word but have never taken the time to balance it out with other aspects. So, accordingly, on the point of scriptural knowledge, there will be all kinds of difference.

Second, there are all kinds of differences in *spiritual experience*. Some people in the Christian Church are babes in Christ. That is not a criticism, it just happens to be a statement of fact. They have relatively recently come to know Christ as Savior and Lord. And their experience of Him is fresh and delightful and exciting, but it is by no stretch of the imagination mature.

On the other hand, we have some very mature people in Christ. The problem with them is that often they are desperately mature and desperately dull—there's no sign of excitement. The freshness is long gone, and they exemplify the stereotypical church in many people's eyes. One man told me that the church is like a banker's dinner—cold and correct, decorous and dead. And a lot of people who are spiritually mature are cold and correct, decorous and dead. Then, a lot of people who are spiritual babes are warm and fresh and exciting, but they don't know what they're talking about. When you put all this together you have the possibility of all kinds of differences. Third, there are differences in *social graces*. There are some people who can handle a discussion and others who can't. Some people can sit down and talk, bring out their differences, and in the end shake hands and agree that neither of them has all the truth and neither of them has assimilated and accumulated all the facts; therefore, probably the sensible thing to do is to agree at that particular point to disagree and not allow the relationship to be strained.

But, there are some people who can't do that, or won't do it. Every little point becomes an issue, every issue becomes a fight, every fight becomes a disaster, and they have one long history of total chaos. When you get this kind of situation in the church, you are going to have differences not only in scriptural knowledge and in spiritual experience, but also in social graces.

Then, of course, fourth, there are differences of *psychological makeup*. Some people really like to have every *i* dotted and every *t* crossed because they feel very uncomfortable if there is any room for flexing. Other people feel totally throttled if there is no room for flexing. The people who want every *i* dotted and every *t* crossed are very careful, very detail conscious, very earnest people indeed. And when they bring this attitude to Christianity, they want chapter and verse for everything. They will stick their fingers in the Bible and say, "show me where it is."

On the other hand, there are people who are more relaxed about the whole thing. They will say, "Well, listen, I can't give you chapter or verse, but there's no question about it. The general principle is there somewhere between Genesis and Revelation."

When a church has different psychological makeups, what happens? Some people, when a difference comes up, are desperately threatened by it. Others, when they come up against threatened people, are unbelievably frustrated with them. This is all it takes to produce all kinds of difference in the church which, if you're not careful, will begin to produce a difficulty.

Difficulties are probable. First of all, difficulties come about because *positions are not clear.* I think we've got to face up to one very simple thing here, and that is that people don't necessarily say what they mean. That is something in which I take great comfort. I certainly hope a lot of things people have said to me were not really what they meant!

There's another thing, of course, that we have to face up to and it is that people don't necessarily hear what you say. Now, if they don't necessarily hear what you say and don't say what they mean, you have all kinds of possibilities, because people's positions may not be very clear at all by the time they have expressed themselves badly or listened inadequately. That, quite frankly, is why there are difficulties in the church. You see, you already have the differences to start with. Then when positions aren't clear, people jump to conclusions and interpret them wrongly.

A result of this, then, is that *perspectives become clouded* as they begin to zero in on this particular issue. They spend more time talking about the issue and, in the end, forget why they are here. We get so wrapped up in the trees that we forget that there are woods and forests on every hand. And that makes a total clouding of the church's perspective very possible indeed.

Then, of course, third, *personalities become involved.* One of the tragic things that happens when differences have been made into difficulties is that personalities become involved. People, not having expressed themselves properly or not having been heard adequately, sometimes begin to attribute motives to those related to the problem. Now, that is one of the most dangerous things that can happen. It is one thing to say, "This is the problem." But when we lose sight of the problem and say, "He is the problem," that is serious.

The situation is made worse when people add, "He is the problem because this is what he is really doing and thinking." By then we have put the issue up so many notches that we are in real trouble. It is very easy for this to happen in the Church of Jesus Christ.

When personalities become involved, and when motives—almost invariably bad motives—are attributed to the personalities involved then you have the fourth problem—*parties are formed.* In Corinth, parties had developed around the powerful personalities. There was the Apollos party, the Peter party, the Paul party and then the super saints, who said, "Well, of course, we're just Christ's people."

This is when you have real trouble, because not only are people not hearing and expressing properly, but now they are arbitrarily identifying the motives of the personalities concerned and forming parties around those people. And before you know what's happened, all the energy of the church is spent in parties combating other parties.

Divisions are possible. When a church gets to the place where parties have been formed, there's a strong possibility that the diverse point in which they were interested becomes more important than the unity of the Body. In other words, in the same way that in the political realm we trend towards single-issue voting, it is possible that in the Church of Jesus Christ people can produce single-issue

When a church gets to the place where parties have been formed, there's a strong possibility that the diverse point in which they were interested becomes more important than the unity of the Body."

reactions. And when these are produced the people are no longer interested in the Body as a whole. They are no longer interested in the balanced life of the fellowship as a whole. Their sole concern is the issue. When this diverse issue becomes more important to them than the unity and life of the whole Body, then the easiest thing in the world is for that person or that group to break off and cause division. That's serious.

There's another factor. Sometimes when we get into these situations egos become involved, then pride becomes involved and statements are made that cannot be retracted. We have taken a position from which we cannot move; we've gone out on a limb and we've sawed it off, and now, because there's no way back, we just decide: "I'm going to keep my pride and my ego intact and take whoever will come with me because my individual pride matters more than the corporate good."

When this happens, the apostle Paul tells Titus: "Avoid foolish controversies and genealogies and arguments and quarrels about the law, because they are unprofitable and useless. Warn a divisive person once and then warn him a second time. After that, have nothing to do with him. You may be sure that such a man is warped and sinful; he is self-condemned."

The Anathema of a Division

Anathema is a Greek word that means something is "utterly condemned, totally unacceptable." Why do we use such a strong word as anathema about a division? Well, first of all, if you identity with a Body of believers and then choose to be part of a division in that Body, you are inflicting an *amputation* on that Body. That's why you should always be careful before you leave a church; that's why you should always be careful before you join a church.

Now, there is a difference between leaving a church in anger or leaving a church over an issue and joining with a group of people to establish a new church. I would call that an organ transplant. There is all the difference in the world between callously amputating a limb and generously donating a member. I believe the latter is permissible and necessary. I believe the former is out of order. The anathema of a division is that the Body of Christ suffers amputation.

Second, the cause of Christ suffers *misrepresentation*. We have plenty of people out there who are ready to be critical about Christians and about the Church of Jesus Christ. Lots of people will have nothing to do with the Church because of our sad history at this particular level. And we have given them all kinds of opportunities to misunderstand who Christ is, what His Church is and what Christians stand for. We should be careful before we ever give our critics opportunity to find fault with us.

Third, disciples of Christ suffer all kinds of *humiliation*. When it comes down to a fight, unfortunately, somebody wins and somebody loses. But in fact, the Church of Jesus Christ loses all around. Why? Because those who win may feel totally justified in the way they handled matters. And those who lose are going to go away hurt, and possibly embittered. There's a real possibility that it's going to take them a long time to get over it. But, remember, they are still members of the Body of Christ. That is why the apostle Paul says to be very careful about this whole business of division in the church.

In 1983 I was asked by *Moody Monthly* to write an article addressing the issue: Is it possible the gifts of women are being buried in the Church of Jesus Christ? I said I thought it was a very real possibility, and I wrote an article accordingly. The article, in turn, generated a number of letters to the editor. Here's a sampling. One man wrote, "In regard to Stuart Briscoe's article, *nonsense.*" A lady wrote, "After reading several of your articles on the role of women, I was so infuriated, I had to sit down and write immediately. Please cancel my subscription."

Now, isn't it nice to have Christians agree? You see, they read the article, and one was so infuriated by it, she said, "Cancel my subscription immediately." The other person reading it said, "Nonsense."

The fascinating point, however, is that although they both disagreed strongly with what I had written they were taking exactly opposite positions.

The difficulty here stems from the differences of approach. Let's face it, there are some people who haven't cracked the Bible on this whole issue at all. I mean by that, there are some people in the Church of Jesus Christ who address the issue of women in the Church on a 100-percent secular basis. And they aren't feminists. Now, I understand feminists and have some degree of sympathy for some of what they are saying. I don't very often have too much sympathy for the way they're saying it, however.

But when people begin to address the specific issues of the Church on a purely secular approach, we've got to accept the fact that with all due respect they may have some degree of truth, but they're not really addressing the issue. On the other hand, there are some people who can stub their fingers in a verse and say, "It says here, let the women keep silence. That's all there is to it." That is not all there is to it, because the same person who wrote, let the women keep silence, also explained under what circumstances they were allowed to break their silence. And the very same person who said, let the women keep silence, also had women who work with him of whom he

approved who did anything but keep silence (see 1 Cor.
14:34).

Now then, some people can take a verse and underline
it until it comes through their maps. They've got their
position. That's it. Other people will take this verse and
that verse and pull the whole thing together and you know
what they'll discover? They'll discover that this thing is far
more complex than they ever thought.

In fact, I would have to say, I believe the gospel of
Jesus Christ is fundamentally simple and intrinsically complex. And the more I study the Word of God, quite frankly,
on most issues the less dogmatic I'm prepared to be.

Now then, if we have differences in approach, differences in psychological reactions to these things, let's face
up to it. Not only do we have women who are addressing
this issue from a purely feminist point of view, we have
men reacting from a totally chauvinistic point of view. Men
say, "Listen, I'm in the business world; I've had it up to
here with striking women and no way am I going to sit and
have them striking in the church. No way. Count me out."

Here's another issue. At Elmbrook, we made a suggestion that people write their government representa-
tives to be alert to and aware of the peculiar and special
needs of the poor, with particular reference to those who
are hungry.

This all came about because the board of deacons, in
its remarkable wisdom sometime ago, determined that
part of Christian mission was concern for the social well-
being of people. Accordingly, they appointed a social concerns committee whose mandate was to identify matters
of moral and ethical significance in which Christians ought
to have a voice, take steps to educate the congregation as
a whole concerning these issues, and make suggestions
how people, if they wished individually, could respond to

those issues. This is what the social concerns committee did and from that some differences were identified. As a result, some difficulties developed and we had to face it, if they weren't handled properly, division could have resulted.

Why? For all kinds of reasons. Some people are conservatives; some people are liberals. It's as simple as that in some issues. Some people have a high view of government and some people think government stinks. That's another reason. But other people have addressed it from the Bible, and have said, "Listen, the Church is to stay out of politics, our mandate is to go into all the world and to make disciples period." And other people say, "That's the Great Commission; what about the great commandment?

The great commandment is that we should love period. Everything is covered by that. Some people say our responsibility is the spiritual well-being of people. Other people say, "Oh, you mean people are just bodiless spirits?" Well, what are people? Are people soulless bodies? Or are they bodiless souls? If they're bodiless souls, then the obvious thing to do is spend time dealing with their souls. If they're soulless bodies, we need to spend time on their bodies. Do they live in isolation? No. Do we then just deal with individuals or do we deal with society? Some say you've got to deal with their bodies, souls and their society, because it's nonsense to talk about an individual apart from society, or deal with an individual as if he doesn't have a body, or deal with him as if he doesn't have a soul. We have to embrace all of these.

We've had some interesting responses to all of this. One delightful anonymous letter suggested a very simple solution to the whole thing: "Cut the pastors' salaries if they're so interested and send that money to feed the poor." Thank you for that thought; and next time sign the letter. Other people were considerably more gracious. Many were extremely thoughtful. Some generated some light; others generated nothing but heat.

It's fascinating being a member of the Church of Jesus Christ, because you've always got differences. If you're not careful, they'll produce difficulties, and if difficulties aren't handled properly, you finish up with a division.

Discipline in the Church Must Not Be Avoided

There have been times in church history when discipline has been exercised with something resembling fiendish delight. We have all been made aware by the critics of Christianity of the excesses of some of our forebears in the administration of church discipline. Burnings at the stake, wearing of scarlet letters, inquisitions have all served to make modern church people decidedly nervous about disciplining their members.

In more recent times the threat of legal action in the courts and the possible resultant crippling damages have made church leaders even more reluctant to deal with their erring members. But the fact remains that if proper discipline is not applied where appropriate, the result will be a marked decline in the spiritual nature of the church and a confusing signal for those who are trying to evaluate the pros and cons of religious experience. Then, of course, there's the loss suffered by the erring believers if they are never taken to task for their behavior, with restoration in mind.

When Is Discipline Necessary?

There are at least three answers to this question. First,

when people disrupt the building of the Body. There are
times when members of a congregation for whatever reason seem to apply themselves to the tearing down of what
other people are trying to build in the name of Christ.
They should be dealt with patiently and carefully with a
view to understanding why they are behaving in such a
manner. But these kinds of people can demand far more
attention than is their due and the time will eventually
come when the leaders of the church determine how much
more attention can and should be given to the person concerned before they are presented with some straightforward alternatives. This kind of discipline requires great
tact and insight, because while we should always be mind-
ful of the individuals, we must also have the well-being of
the Body as a whole in mind.

Second, *when practices corrupt the life of the Body.*
There appear to be an increasing number of cases where
people in the church have been ensnared in immoral situations in their businesses or their private sexual lives. This
kind of situation is deeply embarrassing to all concerned
and as a result the natural tendency is to hope it isn't true
and if it is to assume that it will go away. The problem with
this approach is that when a member of the body engages
in overtly immoral behavior the reputation of the fellowship is inevitably tarnished and, of course, the enemies of
Christ are given yet another opportunity to blaspheme His
name. Therefore, the old blind-eye approach is not good
enough and decisive and caring action must be taken.

Third, *when problems interrupt the ministry of the
church.* It was Paul who admonished all believers to live at
peace with each other but it was he who confronted Peter
concerning his problematic behavior (see Rom. 12:18;
Gal. 2:11). Was he being self-contradictory? No, there
came a time in Paul's estimation when living at peace with

214 Purifying the Church

Peter became secondary to ensuring that the work of the ministry went unhindered. When in his judgment that time arrived he stepped into the situation and the sparks began to fly, although it should be pointed out that the two men apparently remained on good terms after the confrontation. In all ministries there is the possibility that similar decisions will need to be made, but like all disciplinary issues they are by no means easy, and require the greatest of care.

How Is Discipline Administered?

First, *the people concerned are approached* personally. This needs to be stressed because it is far easier to approach someone else rather than the offending person. The intent in the approach is, of course, to "warn" the person presumably about the seriousness of their behavior and possibly with a view to outlining the perceived consequences of what has transpired. This instruction would be designed presumably to outline a series of steps that would be appropriate to remedy the situation, but at the same time there would be a serious statement concerning the necessity for action to be taken by the fellowship, if the proposed remedies are ignored or disregarded. If appropriate responses are forthcoming then reconciliation can begin, but if nothing is achieved, then what?

Second, *the people concerned are approached again.* These instructions should, of course, be read in conjunction with the well-known teaching of our Lord recorded in Matthew 18:15-20. If the pastoral instructions are harmonized with the dominical teachings, the return visit would presumably be conducted in the presence of others who are aware of the problem and who care deeply for the offending people and those who are being offended. It is always hoped at this juncture that if the initial visit was fruitless then the second visit will not only show the depth of concern of the church leaders, but will also show, by the fuller participation of others, that this is a matter to be taken with the utmost seriousness. But what if there is still no response?

Third, *the people concerned are disciplined.* The discipline Titus is required to administer is related to a brand of social ostracism, which would be deeply humiliating and devastating in the days of the early church, even more so than at the present time. In those days there would not be a church on every street corner in most of the Cretan towns, so if the disciplined person was "avoided" and the members of the fellowship "had nothing to do with them" it would be a great disgrace.

Today people often fail to respond in repentance to admonitions, but compound the problem by denying what they have done and simply transfer to another church, which more often than not is not at all interested in why they are no longer attending their previous fellowship. Added to this are the dark threats of legal action and, all in all, a sad state of affairs exists in the modern church when disciplinary action is attempted. However, this does not mean it should be abandoned, because there are always cases of people who, when they are treated firmly and lovingly, do respond and as a result come through the experience richer and more mature. The same can also be said for the church and its leadership when they have sought to discipline properly with a view to honoring the name of Christ, preserving the integrity of the fellowship and seeking to lead the erring one into a deeper knowledge of the Lord.

In the church there is no shortage of hot heads and cold hearts and these do not adorn the gospel. We need cool heads and warm hearts if the church is to be disciplined in order to be discipled.

Questions for further study _____

1. What should the local church be in society? How does God view the local church?
2. What is one thing the apostle Paul says is not accepted in the Church? Review Titus 3:10. How does your church deal with divisive people?
3. Differences lead to difficulties and these in turn lead to division in a church. What accounts for differences in a church? How do these differences lead to difficulties? Why must we be strict in dealing with division in the church?
4. Review the process for discipline in the church, as outlined in this chapter.